NC

# Al-Anon
# Family
# Groups

*formerly, "Living With An Alcoholic"*

*Other books by Al-Anon Family Groups:*

AL-ANON FACES ALCOHOLISM
THE DILEMMA OF THE ALCOHOLIC MARRIAGE
ONE DAY AT A TIME IN AL-ANON (Daily Readings)
FORUM FAVORITES
ALATEEN—HOPE FOR CHILDREN OF ALCOHOLICS
LOIS REMEMBERS (a biography by our co-founder)
AL-ANON'S TWELVE STEPS & TWELVE TRADITIONS
ALATEEN—a day at a time

# Al-Anon Family Groups

*formerly, "Living With An Alcoholic"*

## Al-Anon Family Group Headquarters, Inc.
### NEW YORK ● 1985

Al-Anon Family Groups
© AL-ANON FAMILY GROUP HEADQUARTERS, INC. 1966, 1973, 1980, 1984

Post Office Box 182
Madison Square Station
New York, N.Y. 10159-0182

*Revised Expanded Edition*
*First Printing, March 1966*
*Second Printing, June 1968*
*Third Printing, November 1971*
*Fourth Printing, Revised, May 1973*
*Fifth Printing, July 1974*
*Sixth Printing, January 1976*
*Seventh Printing, September 1976*
*Eighth Printing, Revised, March 1978*
*Ninth Printing, Revised, March 1980*
*Tenth Printing, April 1981*
*Eleventh Printing, November 1982*
*Twelfth Printing, March 1984*
*Thirteenth Printing, February 1985*

Library of Congress Catalog Card No. 84-70191
ISBN-0-910034-54-0

*Approved by*
*World Service Conference*
*Al-Anon Family Groups*

PRINTED IN THE UNITED STATES OF AMERICA

# CONTENTS

*The purpose of this book is to help those who feel their personal lives are being or have been affected by the obsessive drinking of a family member or friend.*

*The light which it sheds on the problem of alcoholism should also be helpful to those who come in daily contact, professionally and socially, with alcoholics.*

God grant me the serenity
to accept the things I cannot change,
courage to change the things I can,
and wisdom to know the difference.

# INTRODUCTION

This is the story of a unique fellowship whose members are people from many lands, of many races, creeds and walks of life. We come together in an inspiring endeavor to help ourselves and others to overcome the frustration and helplessness caused by living or having lived with an alcoholic. We turn to Al-Anon Family Groups to learn how to lead purposeful and satisfying lives.

Al-Anon Family Groups, Al-Anon and Alateen, are a fellowship of families and friends of alcoholics who may still be drinking compulsively, who may have found sobriety in Alcoholics Anonymous or by other means, or who may no longer be part of our lives.

We unite to solve our common problems of fear, insecurity and the warped family relationships associated with the disease of alcoholism.

Those whose loved ones have achieved sobriety often find that life with a *recovering* alcoholic also presents problems of adjustment. For these, too, there is help in Al-Anon.

Like the members of our fellow society, Alcoholics Anonymous, Al-Anon members believe that the way to help ourselves is to share willingly with others what we receive in serenity of spirit and in enriched lives.

# CHAPTER I

# HOW AL-ANON CAME TO BE

In the beginning, AA was a family affair. Parents, mates and children all went along to AA meetings, usually held in somebody's home. Anyone who was still lucky enough to have a home shared it with those without one. So in a very real way Al-Anon had its roots in Alcoholics Anonymous. When the AAs were meeting to discuss their alcoholism and help each other cling to sobriety, the wives would talk over their difficulties. Sometimes these get-togethers were mainly for mutual comfort. Often the wives served coffee and cake to their spouses who were getting together to help each other find a new way of life in AA.

The families soon realized they, too, could use the principles with which their husbands were achieving sobriety. For they, too, were in desperate need of help with *their* part of the problem of alcoholism.

The AA families began to see that their own thinking, actions and attitudes might need changing. They realized they could do a great deal to help themselves and each other. Thus the fellowship which was to become Al-Anon began to take form.

During the pioneering years from 1935 to 1941, these close relatives of recovering alcoholics found that difficult family relationships often persisted even after the alcoholics were sober in AA.

The members of the early groups had learned by experience that it was not only helpful to attend AA meetings but that they needed to apply AA principles to all their affairs. But of greatest importance was the working together in groups. They sought to gain a deeper understanding of what alcohol had done to their partners, and how they could rectify what living with an alcoholic had done to them.

Some groups inevitably fell by the wayside, but a sturdy start was being made in Long Beach, California; in Chicago; Toronto; Richmond, Virginia and in a few other places. Holding fast to the basic AA principles, these groups flourished and encouraged the formation of more and more groups, wherever the need was apparent. Out of these grew still others, until today Al-Anon is doing its work in every corner of the world.

By 1948, 87 individuals and groups had applied for listing in the Directory of Alcoholics Anonymous. But AA was solely dedicated to helping alcoholics achieve sobriety, so the budding fellowship had to learn to establish its own identity.

A Clearing House Committee was formed, composed of relatives of AA members in and near New York City. They worked at first from the home of one member of the Committee, then from an office in what was known as the Old 24th Street AA Club House.

The Committee answered individual inquiries, compiled a Family Group leaflet and made a survey of all the known groups. As the result of a questionnaire sent to these groups, the name *Al-Anon Family Groups* was adopted. The Twelve Steps of Alcoholics Anonymous, only slightly changed, were accepted as the principles by which the members would strive to conduct their lives. The group also authorized the Clearing House to handle Al-Anon's public relations activities.

Magazine articles began to attract public attention to the Al-Anon Family Group movement. As inquiries poured into the office and new groups wrote for help, many volunteers rallied to assist.

Al-Anon soon appeared abroad. By correspondence and monthly newsletter (which was sent also to lone members) the Clearing House brought groups and individuals into contact with each other. An annual world directory was mailed to every group. Additional literature was prepared and made available.

Meanwhile the Twelve Traditions of AA were adapted to Al-Anon's use. They were accepted throughout the fellowship as a framework within which the groups could function in unity and became a guide as important to the groups as the Twelve Steps were to individuals.

By 1954 a new group was being born about every three days and the Clearing House work-load had grown so heavy that a paid staff became necessary. This was made possible by voluntary contributions from the groups. The sale of literature provided an additional source of income.

In order to handle its business and financial affairs more efficiently, the Clearing House Committee incorporated in 1954 as a non-profit unit known as The Al-Anon Family Group Headquarters, Inc. Its books are audited by a certified public accountant and regular financial reports are made available to contributing groups.

The Board of Trustees of Al-Anon Headquarters is assisted by an Executive Committee consisting of volunteers and staff.

In 1957, a teenager whose parents were in Al-Anon and AA began a group for people his own age: it was called Alateen. A year later, there were 31 Alateen groups registered with the Al-Anon Headquarters and an Alateen Committee was established.

In 1961 the first of three World Service Conferences, attended by delegates from all over North America, was instituted on a trial basis. In 1963 this Conference was made a permanent part of the Al-Anon structure. In 1970, the Twelve Concepts of Service, explaining the structure of Al-Anon, came into being. This completed the three legacies:

Recovery—The Twelve Steps
Unity—The Twelve Traditions
Service—The Twelve Concepts

Today, the Headquarters' office is known as the World Service Office (WSO) assisting the more than 24,000 registered Al-Anon and Alateen groups. Of these over 7,000 are in other countries. International growth is continuing at an ever-increasing rate; hundreds of meetings are held in foreign tongues. Neither language nor custom, time nor palce, stand in the way of Al-Anon's work: to help the relatives and friends of alcoholics everywhere to a more serene life.

CHAPTER II

# IS AL-ANON FOR YOU?

Go to any typical Al-Anon Family Group, Al-Anon or Alateen, and you will find a cross section of many kinds of people. A wide range of age, occupation, background and temperament makes for an exchange of rich and varied experience in friendship. Al-Anon is a fellowship of men, women, and children. There are also meetings called Alateen for younger members. The number and availability of all meetings are constantly increasing.

Since Al-Anon has its roots in Alcoholics Anonymous and is closely associated with it, many Al-Anon members have alcoholic relatives and/or friends who have achieved sobriety in AA, but there are also many members whose relatives have not yet found release from their addiction to alcohol.

In recent years a growing number of social agencies, alcoholic centers and clinics, individual doctors, ministers and judges are referring relatives of alcoholics to Al-Anon as a source of help in rebuilding their own troubled lives. The increasing amount of information on alcoholism that reaches the public through press, radio and television also increases the number of relatives of alcoholics who hear about Al-Anon. It is becoming generally understood that Al-Anon's primary purpose is not to try to stop alcoholics from drinking but to help those who have been affected by that drinking lead saner, happier, and more productive lives.

The increased general knowledge about alcoholism fortunately brings many people into Al-Anon at early stages of the alcoholic problem. A generation ago wives and husbands of alcoholics struggled for years through their dreary and sometimes imperiled lives without help. Today thousands of relatives and friends of compulsive drinkers are seeking aid before the effects of someone else's drinking have ruined home life beyond repair or taken their toll of sanity and health.

Not only spouses but parents, lovers and young or adult children of alcoholics are learning that they, too, can find comfort and a sense of security afforded by shared experience with a group.

Among Al-Anon and Alateen members you will find in the fellowship are the relatives or close friends of:

1. an AA member who is leading a consistently sober life.

2. an alcoholic who is trying to overcome his compulsion, but is still suffering sporadic lapses.

3. an alcoholic who refuses help from any source.

4. an alcoholic who is separated or divorced from his family or has died.

Among the first group you will meet members who find they need help in improving their own thinking and attitudes even after their partners have achieved sobriety. These are the people who have adopted the Al-Anon program as a continuing spiritual way of life. Since essential elements are gratitude and sharing with others, they continue their work with Al-Anon in order to help others as they have been helped.

People in the second classification need Al-Anon to help them maintain their strength and to meet the disappointment and frustration of the alcoholic's lapses from sobriety. In Al-Anon, as they grow in understanding of the problem, there is good reason to hope that their improved attitudes will help them to recover from the effects of alcoholism on their own lives whether or not the alcoholic finds lasting sobriety.

The family of the active alcoholic obviously needs Al-Anon in order to learn how to live in spite of the confusions and despairs created by the drinking problem. In Al-Anon they gain confidence in themselves and learn that sometimes even the most stubborn refusal to seek help may change once the family's attitude has changed for the better.

When the alcoholic no longer is a member of the family because of either separation or death, those who feel that their personal lives have been deeply affected by close contact with a problem drinker continue to feel a need for the comfort, support and encouragement of the group. Adult children of alcoholics find that, although they may no longer live with an alcoholic parent, their lives have been affected and Al-Anon can help them in many areas.

# CHAPTER III

# UNDERSTANDING ALCOHOLISM
# THE ILLNESS

After centuries of treating alcoholism as a moral weakness, most present-day medical opinion considers alcoholism a disease which, like diabetes, can be arrested, but not cured. Many of the clergy, too, now accept alcoholism as sickness, not sin.

It may be possible for alcoholics to control their early drinking, but once it becomes obsessive, they are no longer able to control it by themselves. Continuing research may discover a physiological as well as a psychological basis for compulsive drinking. Since alcoholism is a disease, it is useless to blame alcoholics for lack of will power, or to plead with them to stop damaging themselves, their families or their business prospects.

Relatives of alcoholics do not blame themselves either: We know we do not cause the disease and we cannot cure it. We can try to understand that anger and resentment breed anger and resentment, and often provide an excuse for more drinking. Love and understanding are of great help. But a loving, understanding attitude does not mean being permissive or protective. Protecting alcoholics from the consequences of their drinking does not help them; it can prevent their realizing and acknowledging a drinking problem and the need for help. The sooner the alcoholic comprehends the nature of the malady, the sooner recovery may be underway. As members of AA put it, alcoholics must "hit bottom" before they show a real desire to stop drinking. They must be ready to admit they cannot cope with the problem alone. They must want sobriety for themselves, not to please anyone else. Because of the growing knowledge concerning the nature of this illness, the alcoholic today often reaches an emotional or mental point of desperation sooner.

It is exceedingly difficult for those close to an alcoholic to refrain from nagging and pushing; we want to be helpful because we are eager to build constructive lives. Many have found it wise to make a firm resolve not to overprotect alcoholics from the consequences of drinking; this often forces alcoholics to face problems realistically. As long as they can depend on someone to get them out of difficulties, they will not have sufficient incentive to seek help.

## Characteristics of Alcoholics

Authorities agree that many compulsive drinkers have certain characteristics in common, but these do not apply to all.

Alcoholics are likely to be persons of intense, if sometimes brief, enthusiasms. They often try to do too much too fast. They tend to demand perfection in themselves and in others. Frustrated, they may become painfully depressed or overly aggressive. There is a lack of inner stability with which to face life's problems in a realistic manner.

Alcoholics can be attractive and intelligent people. Many hold high ideals, which, however, they seem unable to fulfill in daily living.

Compulsive drinkers often seem indifferent to the destruction they bring on themselves and their families; self-destructiveness is a common characteristic of alcoholics.

They may also show marked dependency. This is indicated by unwillingness to face up to the consequences of uncontrolled drinking. They lean on others, most often a loved one, to get their problems solved, and to be forgiven for what they have done. This particular characteristic can give the family and friends an effective means of helping an alcoholic to *want* sobriety. It we firmly refuse to cover up, if we make no attempt to placate offended third parties and appear to remain unmoved when the alcoholic gets into trouble, he or she will be forced to learn to stand on his or her own feet.

Although continuing researches have uncovered still other alcoholic signposts, it is not important to analyze the causes of drinking. These complex physical, mental and emotional tendencies are beyond the understanding of most of us. What we can do is learn that we are *not* responsible for the illness. We can help by trying to achieve serenity for ourselves by not assuming responsibility for anything alcoholics do. We can learn, in Al-Anon, to grow in compassion and emotional detachment as we realize that alcoholics alone can take the first step toward finding sobriety.

### Alcoholic Progression

Alcoholism is known to be a progressive illness. It never gets better, it can only get worse, until radical steps are taken to arrest the progression.

The alcoholic in our life may be in one of these stages of the illness:

1. At the outset, he or she may be a heavy drinker who has not yet been hurt too badly, or has not hurt others seriously. The drinking may be confined largely to weekends or special

occasions. He may have lost little, if any, time from his job. She may still appear to be in control of her situation. A disturbing factor may be that periods between bouts are getting shorter and the drinking itself heavier. While both may still keep their drinking under some control, they are probably on the way to becoming full-fledged alcoholics.

The periodic drinker is perhaps more baffling to the family than the weekend or occasional drinker. As months of sobriety go by, the family gains reassurance, only to have it shattered for no apparent reason. The drinking phase may be heavy and constant for weeks or months, to be followed once again by a long period of non-drinking.

2. Perhaps he or she has reached the stage where serious problems have begun. He may have lost a job or two and his family life may have become tense and unhappy. She may have *lost* too many hours. They recognize that they should do something about their drinking but refuse to consider seeking outside help. They insist they can handle the problem alone. Meanwhile, the drinking continues to get worse, with increasing damage to home and business life.

3. By now the alcoholic himself may recognize that drinking is a problem he cannot control. There may be ample evidence. His closest personal relationships may have been badly affected. He may have been jailed for brief periods as a result of drunken behavior. He may have lost a succession of jobs. She may neglect her work, the children, and her appearance. At this point the alcoholic often wavers between a sincere desire to stop drinking (usually following a particularly bad spree) and a stubborn resistance to real help.

4. Finally the problem drinkers seem completely lost and beyond recovery. They may have been hospitalized or com-

mitted to institutions or have drifted away from all sense of responsibility, forsaking family, friends and every other aspect of normal living. They are headed toward skid row, or are there already.
5. Beyond this lies insanity or death.

*Prelude to Sobriety*

Two facts deserve emphasis at the outset. The first is that few alcoholics, even those in the condition described under No. 4 above, can be said to be beyond hope. While the alcoholics still retain some ability to comprehend the nature of his or her malady and that they can do something about it, there is reason to hope for their recovery, based on the experience of the many thousand who are now sober in AA.

The second fact is that alcoholism does not discriminate with regard to sex. Both men and women are found in the various categories, including the most serious. Many men recognize their loved one in the drinking patterns described. The consequences of a woman's irrational drinking may be hidden longer than that of a man, but the grave and progressive nature of the illness is common to both.

In order to achieve and maintain sobriety, *the alcoholic must have a desire to stop drinking.*

Understanding of alcoholism and of the alcoholic depends upon accepting the limitations that confront the non-alcoholic in dealing with the problem. Pleading, cajoling, pampering or scolding are never successful. The alcoholic has to "hit bottom" for himself or herself before an effective decision to stop drinking can be made.

Alcoholics may hit mental, emotional, or physical bottoms, or all three. This means they know they cannot cope with the problem alone and are ready to accept help.

Not all alcoholics hit bottom at the same stage of their drinking. Some recognize early that they are on the way to disaster and foreseeing catastrophe, begin seeking help.

Other alcoholics are not so fortunate. They will go farther down the scale in their drinking before they are able to admit that they cannot control alcohol.

This situation is exceedingly difficult for the family member or friend. It is not easy to watch others destroy themselves. It is not easy to wait for the alcoholic to face his or her problem. There is much that the family or friend *can* do. A change in attitude may make a great difference in the situation.

The experience of the Al-Anon Family Groups proves it is never too early and never too late for families and friends to try to do something about this complex, progressive illness by learning to understand how it has effected and continues to effect *their* lives.

# Chapter IV

# UNDERSTANDING OURSELVES

*Before Sobriety*

While those we care about are still drinking, we are acutely sensitive to the hurt they cause us. We may consider them selfish, arrogant, irresponsible and lacking in appreciation of us. We reproach them for the time they spend away from home, for failing in their duties as partners, fathers, mothers or children. We rail at them for their failure to handle money wisely and their lack of concern for the future. We often become self-righteous, and in desperation and bitterness, try to retaliate. These are natural reactions—*until we learn that we are dealing with very sick people.*

Our attitudes may have become negative, cynical or desperate. Some of us lose faith in the goodness of life and faith in ourselves. In our deep discontent, we may become too apathetic to believe in the possibility of a change. Even those of us who try to cling to the spiritual resources of our youth often do so without firm conviction or hope.

These cobwebs must be brushed out of our thinking before we can make a new and successful approach to the problems of living.

We are frequently overwhelmed by self-pity. Life, we think, has been cruel in saddling us with an alcoholic. We forget when the alcoholic was kind and generous. We forget the times he or she has tried to make life pleasant for us. We may be blessed with good health and fine children. Perhaps we still enjoy comforts provided by the industry and ambition of the alcoholic in sober periods. We forget to count our blessings; we concentrate on our burdens.

If we look inward, we may discover we are unconsciously developing a marked arrogance. Because we feel the alcoholic seems so obviously wrong, we may assume that we are infallibly right in our attitudes and decisions. Well-meaning friends and sympathetic public opinion tend to encourage us in this belief. Exerting authority over the alcoholic becomes a habit in large matters and small. Unknowingly, what we intend as loving guidance often turns into thoughtless domination and nagging.

### *After Sobriety

When alcoholics first join Alcoholics Anonymous, they may undergo a miraculous change. Life seems very rosy indeed. What we have hoped for, what we have vainly striven for through the years has now become a reality.

But some of us find our loved one's new way of life in AA brings a fresh set of difficulties, problems which we must learn to solve if a happy home life is to be created.

After a period of sobriety, recovered alcoholics may be ready to resume their responsibilities, but we are not always willing to let them do so. When we begin to examine our own attitudes, we are amazed to see how warped our thinking has become. Running things our own way has become a deeply ingrained habit; we are reluctant to let go.

This creates tensions which might have been avoided through an easy-does-it attitude. Little by little, through Al-Anon, we come closer to being honest with ourselves. We see that many of our defects have little relation to the alcoholism. We may still harbor resentments and unconsciously rebel against the burdens of the past. We may become bitter over the fact that others were successful in helping the alcoholic to stop drinking when we could not. Once an important prop in an alcoholic's life, we may have become merely incidental in recovery. This would present a challenge even to well-adjusted minds!

Some resent the fact that newly-sober alcoholics now labor long and diligently to make up for lost time in business. We may even resent the time spent at AA meetings or in helping other alcoholics who are still drinking.

Finally we come to realize that this attitude of possessiveness has no place in our lives. Once we have faith in our loved ones, we learn to release them to live their lives and to AA activities, though we may still feel as isolated and lonely as we did while the alcoholism was rampant. After the first breathtaking feeling of relief and release from tension when our alcoholics have finally accepted AA, we find ourselves standing alone once more amid the wreckage which alcoholism leaves in its wake.

The way out of our own personal dilemma of loneliness is through Al-Anon. We see how AA helps alcoholics ease their burdens by sharing their experience and problems with others who understand them. Just as such sharing is helpful to alcoholics, so it can benefit all those in the Al-Anon Family Groups.

Similarly, those of us whose alcoholics still refuse help can find inspiration and comfort in the Al-Anon way of life. Although still harassed by an active drinking problem, we find it possible to arrange our own lives more confidently and to create a better emotional climate in our homes. We learn to apply the Twelve Steps to our daily lives, and find that our needs, too, are met by their spiritual depth and wisdom.

When we Al-Anon members talk with one another and exchange ideas, we are able to apply the experience of others to our particular problems. We discover we have just as much to gain from the Steps as the alcoholics have. We find that the alcoholic experience has made us sick, too, and that we need emotional sobriety as much as alcoholics need freedom from alcohol.

*The booklet, *Living With Sobriety: Another Beginning,* shares how members have used the program to handle the difficulties they met along with the joys of living with sobriety.

CHAPTER V

# AL-ANON AND THE FAMILY

Anyone who lives with an alcoholic knows how hard it is to create and maintain a normal family life. The natural tendency is to blame all family problems on the compulsive drinker. Alcoholism certainly does contribute to divorce, juvenile delinquency and mental illness but these conditions exist in countless homes where there is no drinking problem. We propose, therefore, to take a look at family life in general before going on to Al-Anon's role in trying to help some of the situations that may be laid fairly at the door of alcoholism.

Dr. Ruth Fox, former Medical Director of the National Council on Alcoholism, reminds us that:

"The family was originally formed for security and procreation. Today, love and companionship are strong additional motives for marriage. As of old, the family should provide food, shelter and material necessities for its members, and, as of old, it should be a buttress against anxieties, establishing the personal identity of each member as part of a loving, reassuring unit. Other functions of the family include the training of children for their various roles in later life: work, sex, and social and creative development. Fulfillment of sex needs between husband and wife aids in solving conflicts and in building satisfactory self-images as mates who are happy in the performance of their privileges and duties.

"In a well-adjusted family, the normal goals of security, pleasure and self-expression are usually attained without too much conflict. Tolerance of differences, respect for individuality and a sharing of responsibility and authority make for a healthy family life.

"Unfortunately, some of the stresses of modern living make this ideal difficult to attain. The struggle of business competition has changed the role of the father to a large extent. He may not have time or energy to function daily as head of the household as he did a generation or so ago. His fear of economic insecurity may have undermined his old confidence. He may be afraid of other men in business and may carry over this anxiety to his home life. In many homes the father may indeed have become the 'forgotten man'; mother may have become the ruler of the household. She seems strong, self-reliant and aggressive. Actually she may be unconsciously disappointed that she can no longer lean on her husband for authority and shared responsibility in the training of the children and the management of the home. She is often confused and frightened. Unwittingly she may be losing her femininity just as her husband may be losing his masculinity.

"The children suffer under this shift of roles. They often feel unable to look to their fathers for strength and guidance and to their mothers for love and understanding. When displacement of roles causes friction between the parents, the children are caught in family arguments and tension. They feel the need for escape, and they find it in loneliness or by turning away from home entirely to seek companionship in unsupervised and often devious ways.

"If the family becomes too seriously disturbed, it tends to become socially isolated, with the added unhappy result that its members are thrown into too close interaction. Often the mother who is alienated from her husband develops an unhealthy, smothering love for one or more of the children. Then instead of a warm, interdependent group, the family pairs off into warring factions: the men, big and little, line up against the women, or father and daughter close ranks against mother and son."

### Al-Anon for Women

A wife with alcoholism to cope with, however, finds such problems the rule rather than the exception. Deprived of her husband's help by his excessive drinking, the mother must make decisions for the family, assume responsibility for rearing the children, face creditors and perhaps even work outside the home to make up deficiencies in the family income.

The necessity to take over her husband's duties creates resentment and confusion in her. She is overworked, nervously exhausted and perhaps always doubtful of her ability to carry all this responsibility.

The husband, notwithstanding his inability to cope with the problems which have fallen on his wife's shoulders, may resent, however unjustly, that his wife has assumed his male prerogatives, usurped his authority. The children are affected by these shifts in parental roles. They no longer have a father whom they can fully respect nor a mother whom they can unreservedly love. When a boy loses his respect for his father he may turn away from the normal masculine goals and develop dependency and perhaps identification with the mother. When the daughter sees her father in a degraded condition, she may actually sympathize with him and blame her mother for the father's drinking.

The social isolation that occurs in any disturbed family is increased when alcoholism is the chief problem.

## Social Contacts

Social relationships outside the alcoholic's family circle may often be almost as distrubing as those at home. Gross flouting of the conventions brings ostracism, not only of the alcoholic, but of the whole family. When alcoholics constantly break the rules of normal behavior loved-ones find themselves trying to walk a tightrope in a high wind: they may love these people who behave in such outlandish manners and want to defend them against criticism even when their conduct is indefensible. Those who feel most free to criticize are usually family members—the children, parents, and often close friends. These are the people mates need and want to keep close, for only those who are deeply interested will take the trouble to speak openly. Others simply withdraw from the embarrassing situation and avoid contact with the alcoholic's family. And the non-alcoholics, anticipating such rejection, withdraw themselves and the family from social contacts.

The more they withdraw, the more frustrated and lonely they become. It is here that Al-Anon can be helpful. Talking with others who have lived with the same problem brings relief and hope to the bewildered non-alcoholic member of the family.

Al-Anon will help them to realize they did not cause the alcoholism and cannot be expected to cure it. They see that they can and should get back into the world. From the small, sympathetic group of Al-Anon they are prepared to move out into social relationships where they will not be subjected to the criticism they have known in the past.

Sometimes an alcoholic will object violently to a mate making outside friends and undertaking outside activities. In this case one would do well to consult a clergyman, a doctor or members of AA who, because of their own experience, may be able to give courage to do what is best. It is generally agreed that the non-alcoholic achieves a healthier frame of mind by becoming active in areas outside the problem which has absorbed time and concern. An improved attitude may very well result in helping the alcoholic face the problem and seek help.

The more nearly normal one can make one's life, the better it will be for the whole family. Some people are so well able to free their minds from the engrossing problem that they even invite guests to the home, notwithstanding the possiblity of embarrassing scenes created by the alcoholic. If entertaining at home is still not practical, there are many other activities to consider, particularly if there are children and young people to be included. Striving for a normal life may be difficult but giving in to despair will have far more troublesome consequences.

Then, in the happy event that the alcoholic should decide to seek help, the family will be well on the way to a wholesome outlook on life, with many difficult adjustments already made.

### The Sex Problem

Alcoholism often seriously affects the marriage relationship. Approached by a drunken, maudlin or violent spouse, it is not easy to remind oneself that the condition is due to a sickness that should be treated with tolerance and tenderness. When new members come into Al-Anon, they want desperately to know the answer to sex problems. Shyness and loyalty may keep them from stating specific details; and even when members speak freely, friends in Al-Anon do not venture to give advice.

Al-Anon groups are not authorities on marital relations. Members can offer a troubled newcomer assurance that many who have had difficult experiences in this vital phase of their lives have found solutions.

Personal matters of this kind are best discussed privately with an older member of the group.

Whether or not the question of sex comes up for discussion in an Al-Anon group will depend upon the wishes, viewpoint and maturity of its members.

However, a realistic and objective approach to the sex problem may be genuinely helpful to both Al-Anon members and the alcoholics with whom they are concerned. In Al-Anon we can bring out into the open the fears and resentments that have been festering, and learn that they are typical of alcoholic situations rather than isolated cases. Members do not attempt to give specific counsel, but they may be able to clarify the troubled person's thinking, tell of solutions to their own problems if they care to, and suggest professional help for problems beyond their experience.

Increased or decreased sexual drives in the alcoholic spouse may have no real relation to love. Nor can love be gauged by reactions to lack of tenderness or even lack of personal cleanliness which are not uncommon in the uncontrolled drinker. Unfortunately, aversion to a spouse who was drinking, frequently persists even when there is sobriety. Discussions of these matters sometimes reveal need for a time of healing in the relationship; some members may see that they have been rejecting sex as a punishment. They will learn that a more compassionate and understanding attitude toward either of these difficulties may reduce the tensions in the marriage relationship. Promiscuous behavior toward others on the part of alcoholics, while difficult to condone, does not necessarily mean they no longer love their mates. When such actions lead to sordid involvements, medical or legal advice is required. Certainly these situations are beyond the scope of the amateur, however interested and willing to help.

Al-Anon members can nevertheless be a source of comfort

during such periods of stress. Often their understanding makes it possible for the unhappy spouse to defer drastic action.

When a member is faced with a sex problem that threatens a marriage, professional advice can be sought before feelings grow too deep for healing. Spouses sometimes feel that their mate's outrageous behavior when drinking has created a permanent rift in their marriage. Competent counsel may tide over the crisis and do much to help both partners to renew their marriage.

Many an alcoholic has found a happy change in a spouse after there has been an opportunity in Al-Anon to learn a more understanding attitude. The book, THE DILEMMA OF THE ALCOHOLIC MARRIAGE, discusses the Al-Anon program's application to marriage problems.

### Al-Anon for Men

There are differences between the situation facing a man married to an alcoholic and the wife of an alcoholic yet the problem is essentially the same. A man may go to Al-Anon while his wife is still drinking, to learn how to cope with the uncertainties that beset him daily. But just as often a man becomes a member of Al-Anon after his wife is well-established in sobriety. In some cases a man may feel disinclined to give up any more time to his wife's recovery now that she has found an answer to her problem. But if he recognizes that the difficulties the family has suffered are not her problem alone, but his as well, he will see the need for active and continuing participation in Al-Anon.

Some men imagine an Al-Anon meeting as a kind of ladies' group, and certainly he wants no part of that. If despite this feeling he decides to try it anyway, he will learn that Al-Anon members will give him real help and understanding. He will find friends among people who have been through the same agonizing experiences as his. He learns how they rose above their difficulties to live normal, contented lives.

Sometimes the men in an Al-Anon group have considered breaking off to form a stag group because they think other men might better understand the problem. There are a number of such groups around the country. Most groups, however, decide against such separation. In its early years, AA had the same situation in reverse; when nearly all the AA members were men, some women's groups were formed. Over-all experience has shown, however, that much good therapy is missed when groups consist exclusively of men or women.

While the basic problems of mates in Al-Anon are identical, there are some differences:

*Economic:* Husbands are more likely to leave alcoholic wives than the reverse. In many homes, the husband is the bread-winner. The wife of an alcoholic, especially where there are children, will endure incredible hardships because her children and she are dependent upon him for support. He may spend most of his earnings on liquor; bills accumulate; there may be no money for needed clothing and even food—but as long as he provides even a token livelihood, she hesitates to assume that responsibility.

When the wife is the alcoholic, however, the husband resents having his hard-earned income wasted on liquor. He feels his efforts to be a good provider are fruitless. The wife may threaten his career by her irresponsible behavior toward his employer, his clients or his customers. If there are no children and he feels the situation is beyond redemption, he may very well decide to make a new life for himself without his alcoholic wife. If there are children, he may remove them by legal means to a more wholesome environment to protect them from the consequences of the mother's neglect.

*Social:* Both husbands and wives of alcoholics are reluctant to bring guests into the home. The husband has one advantage, however. He can take his friends out and entertain them at restaurants, thus avoiding the uncertainties of his own household and his wife's probable condition.

Visiting other people's homes also presents difficulties. He has no way of knowing whether his alcoholic wife will be able to keep an engagement they have made. And if there should be a promising beginning to a social evening, they may have to leave because of the alcoholic's behavior. When their hosts have been made so uncomfortable that friendship will no longer stand the strain of embarrassment, people simply stop inviting them. This pattern, familiar to the woman with an alcoholic husband, has added to it a certain shame for the man who realizes that other men look down on a husband who cannot control his wife's behavior. He fears he is thought weak and unmanly. When he gets advice from others it isn't generally "Why don't you leave her?" but "What you ought to do is let her know who's boss."

Al-Anon offers more rational ways of dealing with the problem.

Where children are involved it is just as difficult for a man as for a woman to assume the roles of both parents. When the woman is the alcoholic, the whole burden of child raising may rest on the father, and there is the added problem of the children having a drunken mother around the house all day. The time he can spend at home seems never enough to do all the necessary chores: buying food, taking care of the family laundry, finding someone to do the cleaning. Often he must do something about the children, whom he may find huddled in a closed room, too frightened to come out. They may be sick with colds or upset stomachs, with no one to take care of them or call the doctor.

Even after he has brought order out of the chaos he finds awaiting him, he has the discouraging conviction that it will all have to be done over and over again.

Changes may take place in his own attitude toward drinking. If he has been a social drinker, he may tend to drink less and less— or not at all. His wife regards this as tacit disapproval, which may give her still another excuse for drinking.

Once a wife joins AA and stops drinking, both are faced with the slow journey back to normal living. If the husband has been fortunate enough to find Al-Anon, he will discover how seriously he, the non-alcoholic, has been affected by the years of tension and strain. And it is there, in the fellowship of understanding friends who share his problem, that he can learn how to restore family harmony.

The Twelve Steps of AA must become a pattern of living for the husband, as it is for his AA wife. If either one has a "slip" in the early period, it need not be regarded as cause for despair. Al-Anon members may have such relapses, just as alcoholics do.

There may come a time when the non-alcoholic feels he no longer needs Al-Anon. He is weary of what seems to be a rut, and wants a taste of the world where he is not constantly being reminded of the ogre of alcoholism. This may cause a slip, although the cause is relatively unimportant. What *is* important is that the non-alcoholic husband needs Al-Anon, not occasionally but all the time. One man put it this way:

"It has become and must remain an integral part of my life, the frame around the picture that is me. Without it my edges begin to curl, my fabric warps and my paint begins to crack."

Once in Al-Anon, the non-alcoholic husband, like his feminine counterpart, learns to live in the light of certain insights:

First, that his wife is suffering from a progressive, incurable illness.

Second, that while he can do nothing to cure her or to prevent her from drinking, he can help her immeasurably by reaching out to her in love and understanding.

Third, recognizing that he is powerless over his wife's alcoholic problem, that he must learn to live his own life as best he can despite her drinking.

Fourth, that Al-Anon may help him learn to accept this and seek solutions to the major problem.

Fifth, that many problems are not capable of solution without help, and that while some help comes from sharing experiences, the greatest help can come only from a Higher Power. One can learn to surrender to this Higher Power, accepting the fact that life will always present some difficulties but that God never burdens us with more than we can bear.

### Children of Alcoholics

A home with an alcoholic parent is a dreary and difficult environment for children. They are immersed in confusion, groping for security. Unhappy within the home, they are often just as miserable outside it, exposed to taunts from schoolmates and pity from grownups. Fear, lack of sleep and food, and lack of guidance and normal family affection may make children withdrawn or openly hostile.

Parents in Al-Anon begin to learn to adjust to the problem with understanding. The children find attitudes more consistent and dependable. This relieves their confusion and anxiety. They gradually understand that the drinking is not caused by either their own or their sober parent's behavior. Hope is renewed for these youngsters when they discover that the alcoholic is ill. Many are helped to a better understanding of the problem by joining Alateen groups.

The book, ALATEEN—HOPE FOR CHILDREN OF AL-COHOLICS, is specifically for such teenagers.

In recent years there has been a sizeable increase in the number of adult children of alcoholics in Al-Anon, some of whom have made the transition from Alateen. While many no longer live with an alcoholic parent, they still recognize the need for help as their relationships continue to be effected by their past experiences, their lingering fears and resentments.

# CHAPTER VI

# ALATEEN GROUPS

Alateen came into being to fill a need, in much the same way as Al-Anon was born. For years the only source of help for adolescent children of alcoholics was to attend AA and Al-Anon meetings with their parents. Many saw the change that Al-Anon and AA made in their parents and were grateful for the improvement in their daily lives. They learned that the alcoholic in the family was sick and not weak-willed or intentionally unkind. These young people, however, lacked association with others of their age group who understood their particular problems. In 1957, a high school boy in California felt the urge to talk to other teenagers who would identify with his sharing. His story is almost as wonderful as that of the co-founder of AA.

Bob, the son of an alcoholic father, was in serious trouble; he seemed certain to be sent to a school for problem children. His mother, active in Al-Anon, persuaded the school officials to give Bob one more chance. She and her husband urged him to try using the Twelve Steps in his daily life. He began going with his parents to AA meetings, and to Al-Anon with his mother. The meetings helped Bob but he still felt frustrated; these grownup problems weren't his problems. This brought him to the idea of forming a group for teenage children of alcoholics. That was the beginning of Alateen.

Bob was right in believing that teenagers would welcome a

group of their own. Al-Anon and AA members helped this first group of adolescents live through its birth pangs. In less than a year the group grew from five to twenty-three active members. It set the pattern and established basic Alateen procedures that have been followed ever since.

The age range of Alateen groups at first covered the literal thirteen to nineteen bracket; today some groups stretch the limits to include preteens to twenty year olds. Sometimes the larger Alateen groups split so that the younger members meet separately from the older teenagers.

Alateen meetings can be held in another room of the same public building where Al-Anon or AA groups meet, usually at the same time. Some groups meet in school buildings during after-school hours. There are also Alateen meetings held in juvenile homes, hospitals and penal institutions. As the members of the group plan meetings together, they draw comfort and interest from each other. Being part of a group that is definitely their own fills a lonely void.

Every Alateen group must have an active Al-Anon Sponsor who guides the group and helps the members understand the Traditions. An AA may assist the Al-Anon in sponsoring.

Alateen groups become self-supporting through voluntary contributions, but some Al-Anon groups help with the expenses of Alateen until the group has grown enough to pay its own way.

Alateen officers are elected and function just as in Al-Anon. A teenager who may be a frightened and seemingly unimportant member of the family often gains self-confidence as the chairman of the group. Being responsible for opening the meetings by: a moment of silence, reading the Twelve Steps and Twelve Traditions, as many groups do, helps to give the teenager a sense of dignity. Since Alateen is a vital part of Al-Anon's structure, its

Group Representatives are encouraged to attend District and Assembly meetings where they have both voice and vote.

Alateens are cautious about preserving the anonymity of Al-Anon, AA and Alateen members. They are as conscientious as adults about placing principles above personalities.

Alateen is Al-Anon for younger members. It follows the same program and can be a vital link in the family recovery. Alateen meets the needs of young people whose lives have been or are being affected by someone else's drinking. They learn alcoholism is a disease. Alateen helps them to become individuals. In trying to work the Twelve Steps, they are given a new beginning. Faith in a Higher Power, perhaps for the first time, offers peace of mind and a sense of direction.

# Chapter VII

# AL-ANON AND THE COMMUNITY

The community, including its professionals, seems to have made great strides in understanding the disease of alcoholism and its effects on the alcoholic. Newspapers, magazines and television regularly carry stories of programs and research studies. Popular figures in government and the entertainment world talk freely of their battles with alcohol and their recovery from compulsive drinking. There is, however, still little understanding of the effects of that drinking on others.

For many years, Al-Anon Family Groups have played a vital part in widening public awareness of alcoholism as a family disease, offering help locally to the friends and families of alcoholics and providing professionals with an established resource for referrals. Through a concerted public information effort, Al-Anon has helped make people aware of the devastating results on those who have special relationships with an alcoholic: the families and friends.

Because they care, those who are close to alcoholics, are caught up in the behavior of another person. They react to the drinking, they are ashamed of public scenes and become obsessed with what the alcoholic is doing while they worry about *everything* and make excuses for the alcoholic. Sooner or later, their anxiety turns to anger. They realize they have been stuck with too many responsibilities and they want to strike back, punish the alcoholic for the hurts and frustrations caused by uncontrolled drinking.

Then they begin to pretend, especially to themselves. They accept the promises, they want to believe the problem has gone away even when every good sense tells them there is something wrong. This denial keeps the family and friends from seeking help for themselves for years while they try to contend with a constant nagging guilt for a disease which they did not cause, and which they cannot cure.

These are the people who bring their despair to their community. These are the neighbors who cannot concentrate on their health because they are thinking about someone else's drinking; these are the children who cannot pay attention in class because they are overwhelmed by their family situation; these are the workers who are chronically absent from their jobs; they need help.

That families need help cannot be stressed too strongly; they are deeply affected. It is with the help of Al-Anon that they learn to ease their emotional burdens by sharing their experience, strength and hope with others. In meetings within their own community, they have the opportunity to learn where their responsibilities lie, to discover self-worth and to grow spiritually. In Al-Anon, the emphasis begins to be lifted from the alcoholic and placed on their own recovery.

In searching for help, the family discovers that Al-Anon is not a professional fellowship nor is it a religious organization. It is not a counseling agency nor a treatment center and it is not allied with any other organization offering such services. What they do find is an independent fellowship which neither endorses nor expresses opinions on outside issues. No dues or fees are required and membership is voluntary; yet under these very special traditional guidelines, Al-Anon manages to cooperate with those in the fields of education, law, medicine, religion and industry.

Al-Anon works with the community toward a common goal by offering the *availability* of a program rather than promoting its *use*. Through the media, through participation in local and national events, exhibits, magazine articles, films, speeches, posters, books and other literature, Al-Anon informs the community that it is available to those who feel their lives have become unmanageable because of someone else's drinking. Many of Al-Anon's members are introduced to the program of recovery through a third party; a member of the clergy, a social service worker, a doctor, an employer, a counselor, or perhaps, a member of the court. These professionals understand that members of the family and friends of alcoholics have suffered from the effects of the disease of alcoholism and need help in solving common problems with others like themselves who have lived in similar situations. Most professionals who refer their clients to Al-Anon and Alateen groups believe Al-Anon provides a daily support system, one which they could not hope to match in time or attention, in spite of their training. They are content to pursue their own particular theory of recovery in their private sessions, and recommend Al-Anon and Alateen as a supplement to their care.

On occasion, the Al-Anon acceptance of referrals from professionals may be misunderstood. Interested professionals who are anxious to cooperate, may ask, or be asked to go to Al-Anon or Alateen meetings and may use their attendance to encourage members to recommend their services to others. They are most sincere in their efforts to assist in family recovery and usually they are not aware that Al-Anon groups cannot endorse nor recommend them in return.

It takes tact and kindness to explain that community services are able to specifically recommend Al-Anon and Alateen while the reverse is not so. It might appear that it is a one-sided approach by others in the community but there are several good reasons why Al-Anon does not refer its members to any particular organization.

Al-Anon took its lead from Alcoholics Anonymous. The founders of AA recognized that the unique nature of their program necessitated keeping the fellowships' goals in focus. Those who founded AA knew from experience that AA worked where all else had failed. They wrote down how they had stayed sober and pledged themselves to keep carrying that message to others. They developed a series of ideas which they suggested could be traditionally followed to keep their recovery in mind.

The founders of Al-Anon were fortunate. They were able to observe AA's progress for several years. They concluded that the program was most successful when the Twelve Traditions were observed by the groups. They knew there would be pressures from many sources to adjust and adapt Al-Anon principles to fit a particular recovery theory or blend with a religious view. They strongly resisted such pressures knowing it was not in their best interest to endorse or oppose other views, but to provide a program of spiritual recovery which would be available to those who sought it.

While Al-Anon does not make referrals, its members do understand that they may have needs which Al-Anon cannot fill. Because it does not offer child care centers, legal advice, religious counseling, financial, psychiatric or medical assistance, its members must often seek other community assistance to deal with the confusion and disruption alcoholism brings to the alcoholic and the family.

Al-Anon cooperates in other ways; through its World Service

Office and through local groups, thousands of requests for information are filled. Inquiries are often forwarded to local information services or Area officers who help people reach a group. Where those who ask for help are institutionalized or unable to attend meetings away from a facility, Al-Anon and Alateen members will bring the meeting to them. While the group may have formed at the request of those in charge of the facility, its Institutions meetings are always started and conducted by *Al-Anon* members and may be found in hospitals, courts, mental health facilities, penal institutions and juvenile homes. These meetings may be limited to prospective members or held as open orientation for all who are interested. Often, it is the Al-Anon members who are able to project warmth and understanding which provide newcomers with the incentive to return and encourage them to continue attending *regular* meetings near their homes.

Many regular Al-Anon and Alateen groups hold *open* meetings which can be attended by those in the community who are interested in learning about the effects of alcoholism on the family. At these special meetings, members may give a first-hand account of their changing attitudes in a positive direction, demonstrating emotional growth along with an air of stability.

Al-Anon also cooperates with Alcoholics Anonymous. While members may not have a relative or friend who is a member of AA, there are several ways in which the two fellowships enjoy a special relationship at the same time maintaining separateness and individuality.

CHAPTER VIII

# *THE TWELVE STEPS

These Steps are used by members of Alcoholics Anonymous to achieve sobriety and spiritual growth. They were adopted by the Al-Anon fellowship for the enlightenment and guidance of its members.

So universal was the inspiration by which the Steps were originally written that Al-Anon, in adapting them to its use, changed only a single word: in the Twelfth Step, the word *alcoholics* became *others*.

1. We admitted we were powerless over alcohol—that our lives had become unmanageable.
2. Came to believe that a Power greater than ourselves could restore us to sanity.
3. Made a decision to turn our will and our lives over to the care of God *as we understood Him.*
4. Made a searching and fearless moral inventory of ourselves.
5. Admitted to God, to ourselves and to another human being the exact nature of our wrongs.
6. Were entirely ready to have God remove all these defects of character.
7. Humbly asked Him to remove our shortcomings.

*An in-depth look can be found in the book, AL-ANON'S TWELVE STEPS & TWELVE TRADITIONS.

8. Made a list of all persons we had harmed, and became willing to make amends to them all.
9. Made direct amends to such people wherever possible, except when to do so would injure them or others.
10. Continued to take personal inventory and when we were wrong promptly admitted it.
11. Sought through prayer and meditation to improve our conscious contact with God *as we understood Him,* praying only for knowledge of His will for us and the power to carry that out.
12. Having had a spiritual awakening as the result of these Steps, we tried to carry this message to others, and to practice these principles in all our affairs.

These Steps have such vast spiritual implications that whole books could be written about them. Here is a brief analysis of each:

### STEP ONE

*We admitted we were powerless over alcohol—that our lives had become unmanageable.*

It may be difficult to admit we are not sufficiently strong, or wise, or determined to conquer the problems that confront us. We may think our difficulties can be overcome by trying to control or stop the alcoholic's drinking.

We may still believe we can change the irrational behavior of an alcoholic husband, wife, son, daughter or parent.

We begin our recovery when we bring ourselves to realize we are trying to control something that is beyond our powers: *alcoholism;* that we are just as powerless as the sick and troubled drinker is to bring about a change by force of will alone.

Can we dare to look at ourselves? Can we admit we are help-less? Once we do, the door to a new way of life is open to us. Humility and surrender can open the way to new strength and liberation from the problems alcohol has brought into our lives.

This First Step is the cornerstone of the entire program.

## STEP TWO

*Came to believe that a Power greater than ourselves could restore us to sanity.*

In taking the First Step we are prepared to believe that we must look beyond ourselves for help in solving our baffling difficulties. We have admitted that alone we are helpless to change our lives.

Step Two challenges us to make another admission: *that the way we have been thinking, acting and living was not reasonable or sane*. This is another step in establishing humble surrender, prerequisite to hope and help. Our self-will may say: "But *I* am sane. I'm not the drunk in my family. I keep the household going, I pay the bills, I try to keep this alcoholic sober." What seems sane and right to us while we are frantically trying to cope with an alcoholic problem will look very different to us when we have acquired a new point of view. This comes to us when we acknowledge a Power greater than ourselves.

For some of us, this is God, the representation of infinite power, wisdom and love. Our task is to realize that *asking* prayers and lip service are not enough to remake our lives.

Some may not call this power, "God." Nevertheless, life experience may have demonstrated to them that there is something higher than nature and behavior. Whatever this power may be to us, we can turn over our despair and unhappiness and ask for help. In surrendering self-will to this Power, we are ready for the next Step.

### STEP THREE

*Made a decision to turn our will and our lives over to the care of God as we understood Him.*

With Step One, we have admitted we are powerless over alcohol and the havoc it has wrought in our lives. If we have accepted Step Two, we have acknowledged that there is a Power stronger and wiser than we are. Now we are ready to turn over our will and our lives to that Power.

What does this mean? We are saying: "I can't handle this problem by myself, God. I need You to guide me. Tell me what to do and I will do it." This is surrender with no reservations. It rules out telling Him, as so many of us do, what we want Him to do for us, and when, and how. It means we can "listen for His voice" and accept His guidance, whatever it may me.

Unhappy people by the thousands have come into the Al-Anon fellowship asking but one boon: sobriety for the alcoholic. And all those who have achieved serenity and a clearer vision have learned that this is *specifying what we want our Higher Power to bring about*. Once we have given our problem into another's hand, we can leave it there, making no stipulations. We have already proved to ourselves that our difficulties are beyond us. Our only hope for peace of mind lies in turning our will and our lives over to God as we understand Him.

*STEP FOUR*

*Made a searching and fearless moral inventory of our-
selves.*

A Fourth Step inventory helps us to take an honest look at
ourselves as we really are. We have so long been preoccupied
with the faults of the alcoholic that we may not recognize our
own. It is hard to acknowledge that we may not be models of
goodness and self-sacrifice.

An honest moral inventory may be difficult and disturbing,
but it is a vital step in our progress. The words *searching* and
*fearless* are significant. They suggest we can track down in their
hidden corners such faults as resentment, fearfulness, bad
temper, self-pity, self-righteousness, impatience and intolerance.
If we are afraid to admit them even to ourselves, we bar the way to
improvement. But once they are uncovered there is room for such
qualities as loving kindness, tolerance, serenity and true
helpfulness.

This need not be an exercise in self-condemnation! Many of us
are already burdened with guilts that may or may not be realistic.

Some of us started by reviewing, for example, everything we
did the day before and making notes. We included the things we
approved of as well as those we condemned in ourselves. These
may have been personal characteristics or long established habit
patterns which were hard to recognize.

As we went into this personal inventory, we found many things
falling into place, illuminating some of the difficulties we were
living with.

The immediate benefit of the inventory was that our thoughts
were fully occupied by the effort to concentrate on our *own* virtues and shortcomings, leaving little time for taking critical in-

ventories of others, especially the alcoholic's.

Its continuing benefit was that it served as a blueprint for progress. It may be difficult to get to know oneself, but the rewards are satisfying beyond belief.

### STEP FIVE

*Admitted to God, to ourselves and to another human being the exact nature of our wrongs.*

The preceding Step is concerned with the searching process, the self-examination inspired by our earnest desire to learn how we have wronged others, and how we have hurt ourselves in the process. Taking Step Five puts into action what we have learned about ourselves.

Taking our own inventory is a painful challenge to our capacity for humility. We may now find ourselves hampered by a natural impulse to *justify* the faults we have found. This is a danger; admitting them not only to ourselves, but to God and another person, can be of immeasurable help in finding ways to eliminate our faults.

We can consider one common fault: self-pity. Living in a situation in which everything is distorted by alcoholism, we are prone to believe that the drinker is to blame for all the calamities that befall us. Working with Step Four may show us we are feeling sorry for ourselves, but we consider we have good reason to be; we find it difficult to believe we are responsible for any part of the situation.

Perhaps the family is saddled with debts. We feel we are entitled to a better life, freedom from worry and confusion. Self-pity, more than any other fault, stands in the way of our spiritual progress. If we accept a kind of life we don't like, perhaps it's because we unconsciously crave punishment for deeply buried guilt feelings we don't even recognize. We are *not* forced to accept life on the alcoholic's terms. There are happier and more rewarding ways to live if we take steps to change our own attitudes. If we realize that the choice is ours, we have no reason for self-pity.

We don't need to take on the emotional responsibilities for the alcoholic's debts. They are his problems. He may be forced to face them if we adopt a "hands off" policy and let circumstances compel him to assume his responsibilities.

If we use this method of analyzing the reasons for our fault of self-pity, we can learn to dissect our other wrong attitudes in the same way. To sum up the pattern of such analysis: We recognize the fault. We may seem to feel the fault is justified. We examine it closely and learn that, even if we *can* justify it, we can make ourselves strong enough to correct it.

Acknowledging our faults to ourselves is not easy, but it will lighten the burden. The next step is to admit these faults to God. If we do this freely and honestly, we find further relief. The final step is to admit the fault to another human being, perhaps an understanding friend in the Al-Anon group.

The dictum that "honest confession is good for the soul" is deeply rooted in centuries of religious philosophy. In modern times it has become the therapeutic procedure in psychiatric treatment. The skillful analyst is always on the receiving end, listening while we unburden ourselves of hidden guilt and confusion.

There is still another element of help in this Fifth Step. When we admit our faults, it is much easier to forgive ourselves for them. We have the consolation of having done something brave and honest; in admitting our shortcomings we make a tacit agreement with ourselves to correct them.

Once we have admitted to ourselves, to God and to another person that we have been resentful and self-pitying, that we have tried to punish those who have hurt us, have condemned another without understanding, and have been short-tempered and irritable even with those we love, we will have taken a big step toward banishing those destructive patterns of thinking and behavior.

### STEP SIX

*Were entirely ready to have God remove all these defects of character.*

We may admit our faults and determine to correct them. But being human, we are still tempted to cling to old ways of thinking and acting. Confronted with the same crises, the same irritations, frustrations and despairs that have always aroused our anger and reproaches, it is hard to maintain poise and tolerant quiet.

In this, too, we are powerless to change things without the help of a Higher Power.

The key word in this Step is *ready*. Do we really want to improve? Are we ready to root out the faults we have acknowledged to ourselves, to God and to another person? Unaided, it is an almost impossible task. You may remember that Benjamin Franklin set himself to removing his shortcomings one by one, concentrating on each fault until it was overcome. We can do this, too. But improvement is much more likely if, at the same time, we consciously establish close contact with God and use it, hourly and daily. Deeply ingrained habit patterns are hard to root out without this help; we cannot rely on our faltering human powers alone.

Once we are wholly ready to have God help us remove our defects, the Sixth Step really works. Results begin to show in our greater ability to accept our difficulties serenely and take wise and constructive action.

### STEP SEVEN

*Humbly asked Him to remove our shortcomings.*

This Step is the climax of our effort to improve ourselves. If our work with Steps Four, Five and Six—the *search,* the *admitting* and the *making ready*—have been deep and thorough, self-will has been relinquished somewhat in favor of God's will. We know He is ready, has always been ready, to help us. Now we come to Him in humility, bringing Him our freely-acknowledged faults to be removed.

Humility is a greatly misunderstood quality. It is not weakness; it is strength. It does not mean submission, resignation or compliance; all these imply that we still have lurking reservations about giving in. In humility there is total willingness to accept God's help because we have finally been convinced that without it we cannot achieve our goals.

This surrender to God's will has miraculous power to bring our lives into order and serenity, and to remove, along with our shortcomings, the causes of our distress and failure.

Asking Him to remove our faults is prayer at its best. It asks, and at the same time it promises, that we are ready to accept His help in eliminating our faults. This also implies a promise to use our God-given honesty and intelligence in solving our problems. In this way we are helped to observe our faults as they may be revealed in day-by-day lapses, so we can correct them at once.

### STEP EIGHT

*Made a list of all persons we had harmed, and became willing to make amends to them all.*

The faults we have been discussing through the preceding four Steps clearly concern *our relationships with other people.* Perhaps we have resented what others have done, or have not done. We've felt sorry for ourselves, allowing intolerance to blind us to the good in others. We have retaliated, punished and denounced, misled by our own self-righteousness. We may have fallen into the habit of lying, often deluding ourselves into thinking it was to protect another. Unreasonable bitterness and irritability may have aggravated our troubles.

This overwehlming guilt for what we have done to others reacts upon us with a terrible toll. Out of this may grow our almost unendurable sufferings.

What can we do about it? Step Eight helps us to get rid of this burden, to free ourselves to be what we *can* be by listing all those we may have harmed, and by being willing to make amends.

Willingness to make amends is a giant step toward making a fresh start with our lives. No one would attempt to write a coherent message on a slate already covered with other writing. It must first be wiped clean and then a fresh start made.

We can begin by forgiving ourselves, the person we have harmed through self-hatred, resentment, recrimination and neglect.

Among others we may have harmed is the alcoholic. We try to realize how he may have suffered from our martyr-like attitude, our criticism and nagging. We recall times when anxiety and despair made us irritable with our families and friends. We may have resented their attachment to the alcoholic, considering it a kind of betrayal. We failed to appreciate their unquestioning, uncritical love for a parent, regardless of his faults.

Perhaps our attitudes have estranged relatives and friends, and even counselors who tried to help us.

All these, and any others whom we may in some way have harmed in our confusion and desperation can be listed in our review of those to whom we wish to make amends.

## STEP NINE

*Made direct amends to such people wherever possible, except when to do so would injure them or others.*

The AA book *Twelve Steps and Twelve Traditions* says of this Step: "Good judgment, a careful sense of timing, courage and prudence—these will be needed when we take Step Nine."

Where estrangements have happened between us and relatives or friends, we can express regrets for what *we* have done. Even if we were not wholly at fault in a disagreement, we lose nothing by apologizing for our part in one.

If somehow we have taken advantage of another person so as to cause them a loss, let us carefully consider how to make up for it, at the same time tactfully avoiding anything that may embarrass another.

Although we may recall exactly how we have injured others, it is not always wise to reopen old wounds. Sometimes it is well to avoid dwelling on the past. We can better make amends by changing our attitude today to one of consistent kindness and compassion.

The purpose of Step Nine is to free our own consciences without reviving the situations that created the difficulties.

### STEP TEN

*Continued to take personal inventory and when we were wrong promptly admitted it.*

Step Four suggests making a study of our shortcomings. We recognized our faults, and in subsequent Steps we tried to do something about removing them. If these Steps were taken in depth, we found real release and comfort in our soul-searching. Perhaps we sighed with relief and said: "Well, that's that, thank goodness!"

When we reach Step Ten, however, we find we have undertaken a lifelong program of improvement. The search for peace of mind and happiness requires continuing self-examination and correction.

Daily vigilance and review are a small price to pay for what we get in this way of life. Many members of Al-Anon have established the habit of taking a daily inventory of their attitudes and actions. Immediate acknowledgment of our errors keeps the slate clean and keeps us prepared to make each tomorrow better than today.

The daily review is by no means a self-condemning procedure, concentrated on shortcomings and mistakes. It is a kind of balance sheet on which we also give ourselves credit for what we have done well, for improvements we observe, and for approval we have received from others.

In addition to the daily inventory, many people find the so-called spot-check a useful tool. For example, if someone offends us and we become indignant, part of the fault in this dissension is ours. If we recognize it at once and quietly try to effect an understanding, we have again cleared the slate and freed our minds and our hearts of the burden of resentment.

The continuing inventory is necessary to our continuing growth.

### STEP ELEVEN

*Sought through prayer and meditation to improve our conscious contact with God as we understood Him, praying only for knowledge of His will for us and the power to carry that out.*

We establish a conscious contact with God by prayer and meditation, whatever our understanding may be of this Power which is beyond our human comprehension. Together they represent an ardent wish for awareness of His presence in our lives. They suggest deep concentration, and for this we need to allot some time when we can be alone with our thoughts.

The purpose of praying and meditating is to keep our minds receptive to guidance. This inward "listening" can guide our thoughts and actions, can bring us peace and confidence that God will make His will known and provide us with the power to carry it out.

### STEP TWELVE

*Having had a spiritual awakening as the result of these Steps, we tried to carry this message to others, and to practice these principles in all our affairs.*

This Step confidently assumes that our earnest efforts to use the Steps as our way of life has brought us a spiritual awakening. This can take many forms. It may come like a flash of revelation, showing us that life has design and purpose and that we have a major role in it. Or it may take place as a gradual change in which we acquire a spiritual sense that illuminates every thought and action.

A spiritual awakening can come to us whether or not we are oriented to a particular religious faith. It makes us able to perceive, feel and believe with a conviction wholly new in our experience. A sudden insight may appear as a new approach to the solution of a problem. This awakening brings with it increased capacity for honesty, unselfishness and love in all areas of daily living. It gives us access to a new source of understanding and strength. We find we have been placed, through our willingness, on a new plane of consciousness.

When this change takes place, we find we have become channels for carrying the message of hope to others who are still fruitlessly fighting the enemies that once were ours. This is the Twelfth Step in action.

Twelfth-Step work in Al-Anon means helping the families and friends of alcoholics, exchanging experiences with others at Al-Anon meetings, offering our services as volunteers in Al-Anon's work and in general taking every opportunity to spread the message of Al-Anon to those who are trying to recover from or learn to live with the problem of alcoholism.

CHAPTER IX

# THE TWELVE TRADITIONS

Just as the Twelve Steps guide the individual in his striving for personal growth and spiritual development, so the Twelve Traditions state the group purposes and principles. Group experience indicates that the unity of the Al-Anon fellowship depends upon adherence to these Traditions:

1. Our common welfare should come first; personal progress for the greatest number depends upon unity.
2. For our group purpose there is but one authority—a loving God as He may express Himself in our group conscience. Our leaders are but trusted servants; they do not govern.
3. The relatives of alcoholics, when gathered together for mutual aid, may call themselves an Al-Anon Family Group, provided that, as a group, they have no other affiliation. The only requirement for membership is that there be a problem of alcoholism in a relative or friend.
4. Each group should be autonomous, except in matters affecting another group or Al-Anon or AA as a whole.
5. Each Al-Anon Family Group has but one purpose: to help families of alcoholics. We do this by practicing the Twelve Steps of AA *ourselves,* by encouraging and understanding our alcoholic relatives, and by welcoming and giving comfort to families of alcoholics.

6. Our Al-Anon Family Groups ought never endorse, finance or lend our name to any outside enterprise, lest problems of money, property and prestige divert us from our primary spiritual aim. Although a separate entity, we should always cooperate with Alcoholics Anonymous.

7. Every group ought to be fully self-supporting, declining outside contributions.

8. Al-Anon Twelfth-Step work should remain forever non-professional, but our service centers may employ special workers.

9. Our groups, as such, ought never be organized; but we may create service boards or committees directly responsible to those they serve.

10. The Al-Anon Family Groups have no opinion on outside issues; hence our name ought never be drawn into public controversy.

11. Our public relations policy is based on attraction rather than promotion; we need always maintain personal anonymity at the level of press, radio, TV and films. We need guard with special care the anonymity of all AA members.

12. Anonymity is the spiritual foundation of all our Traditions, ever reminding us to place principles above personalities.

### TRADITION ONE

*Our common welfare should come first; personal progress for the greatest number depends upon unity.*

This guide suggests that every decision and every action taken by a group has an ultimate effect on the group as a whole. Will it promote growth and unity? Will it extend Al-Anon's help to the troubled families of alcoholics?

Unity of understanding and purpose give the best assurance of growth for the group and for each individual.

This Tradition suggests we evaluate every question with an open mind, taking into consideration each member's views. We may, of course, speak and act freely as our personal experience and conscience dictate, and everyone's ideas should be welcomed as a basis for discussion, for freedom of opinion and expression are nowhere greater than in Al-Anon. Differing views can be resolved by tolerant understanding and mutual respect. Nothing in Al-Anon is more important than our common welfare and the unity of the fellowship—as a group and as a whole.

### TRADITION TWO

*For our group purpose there is but one authority— a loving God as He may express Himself in our group conscience. Our leaders are but trusted servants; they do not govern.*

Continuing the thought of the first Tradition, the second affirms that personal authority has no place in Al-Anon.

When we elect or appoint a leader—whether it be a chairman, a Delegate, or a committee member, whether in a group or the World Service Office(WSO), it confers an opportunity to serve, not to dominate. Individual members are guided by the group conscience, which in turn is guided by a Higher Power whose help we ask in arriving at sound decisions and solutions.

This emphasis on the absence of personal power is intentional in Al-Anon, just as it is in AA, which is also a fellowship of *equals*. AA has achieved worldwide recognition as a means to heal and help. It does so by avoiding domination by individuals.

In Al-Anon we are drawn together by a shared problem. The experience we share levels all differences of background, education, religious and political beliefs, color, race or age. No member is more important than another. The most humble and unlettered, speaking from the heart, may say the very words that finally bring light to someone of far greater intellectual attainment.

Al-Anon members of longer experience usually do guide beginners and help to establish these newer members in group activities. But early leaders wisely retire to the sidelines when newcomers are ready to serve as group officers. Rotation of office provides everyone with an opportunity to serve and sustains interest in the group and its work.

Sharing of responsibilities, insistence or personal equality, promote the development of what we call the "group conscience."

When problems arise, as they often do in human relations, no one member has the right to make a decision for the group. Individually and together, the members seek to be guided by a Higher Power to the decision that will achieve the greatest good for the greatest number.

### TRADITION THREE

*The relatives of alcoholics, when gathered together for mutual aid, may call themselves an Al-Anon Family Group, provided that, as a group, they have no other affiliation. The only requirement for membership is that there be a problem of alcoholism in a relative or friend.*

As simple and clear as this Tradition is, questions of eligibility frequently arise in groups. Serious disagreement may even threaten the unity of the group. Some simple answers are discussed in the next chapter, *"Aplication of the Twelve Traditions."*

The fact is that *anyone* who has a relative or a friend with an alcoholic problem may join Al-Anon, or, together with others, form an Al-Anon group. No person who has this problem may be refused membership.

An important element of this Tradition is the statement that "as a group, they have no other affiliation." This does not interfere with any outside interests of the individual, in political, religious, social or business fields. It does close the door on any affiliation *as a group* with other activities or causes, however worthy of support.

### TRADITION FOUR

*Each group should be autonomous, except in matters affecting another group or Al-Anon or AA as a whole.*

The statement that "each group should be autonomous" appears to offer unlimited liberty for each group to do as it pleases. And so it may, in the conduct of its internal affairs, its way of setting up programs and meetings and how it manages its funds.

This Tradition does withhold the right to do anything that might harm another group, or that gives an unfavorable or inaccurate image of Al-Anon or AA as a whole.

In this Tradition, we who are dedicated to helping those afflicted with a common problem, are asked *to be obedient to the unenforceable*. There is no police force or management group to say: "This you must not do." There is no one who has the authority to punish even those who unwisely do things that damage the reputation of our fellowship. All of us are governed by our own concern for the well-being of Al-Anon, always ready to express our gratitude by conforming to what is best for the group and the fellowship as a whole. We are motivated by our desire to keep Al-Anon strong and growing, and extending its healing help throughout the world.

Although we are autonomous, we are controlled by our own sense of what is fitting and right for the best interests of all Al-Anon and Alateen.

## TRADITION FIVE

*Each Al-Anon Family Group has but one purpose: to help families of alcoholics. We do this by practicing the Twelve Steps of AA ourselves, by encouraging and understanding our alcoholic relatives, and by welcoming and giving comfort to families of alcoholics.*

This is a clear and unmistakable statement of Al-Anon's reason for being, bearing out the statement in Tradition Three that Al-Anon groups should have no other affiliations.

Implicit in this Tradition is the recommendation that we concentrate all Al-Anon activities on our primary purpose: to engage in a program of mutual help with others who are confronted with the problem of alcoholism in someone who is important in their lives.

It suggests we accomplish this by improving our own outlook, character and conduct through study of the Twelve Steps. It tells us that concentration on the Al-Anon program can help us solve our problems.

## TRADITION SIX

*Our Al-Anon Family Groups ought never endorse, finance, or lend our name to any outside enterprise, lest problems of money, property and prestige divert us from our*

*primary spiritual aim. Although a separate entity, we*
*should always cooperate with Alcoholics Anonymous.*

This is an extension of Tradition Five, stating in detail that we do not support—financially or by endorsement—any other cause. Careful observance of this Tradition protects us from dissension. It suggests that dividing our interests can only dilute our effectiveness in the program we have undertaken as a group. If we lend our endorsement to other causes, we are assuming a group responsibility for something that may have little or nothing in common with the Al-Anon program. If we support them financially, Al-Anon may be deprived of funds needed for widespread Twelfth-Step work to help others who need Al-Anon.

This Tradition also points out that we are not affiliated even with so close a relative as Alcoholics Anonymous, although in gratitude for the help it has given us as individuals and as a fellowship, we owe it our complete loyalty in all matters affecting its reputation and well-being.

### TRADITION SEVEN

*Every group ought to be fully self-supporting, declining outside contributions.*

This Tradition applies not only to groups, but to Al-Anon as a whole. As a matter of principle the entire fellowship is self-sustaining.

Accepting contributions from people who are not affiliated with Al-Anon, however well-intentioned their offers of help may be, can lead to compromises with interests other than those of Al-Anon.

All support of Al-Anon activities is derived from contributions at meetings. The funds are used for the needs of the group itself—to pay for a meeting place, for refreshments and for Al-Anon Conference-Approved Literature for use at meetings and to be distributed to new and prospective members.

If there is an Al-Anon Information Service (Intergroup), the groups in the local area usually share the cost of maintaining an office to which people can telephone or come when they need help.

Group contributions also help support the work of the Al-Anon World Service Office (WSO) which acts as a clearing house for the fellowship.

An annual contribution is also made by each group toward the cost of sending a Delegate to the World Service Conference.

All contributions—by members to their groups and by the groups to Information Services (Intergroups), World Service Office and the Area WS Assembly—are voluntary. The group conscience decides how these various activities are supported.

The strong bond which unites all elements of Al-Anon is their interdependence. Groups look to the WSO and Information Services for cooperation and service which they in turn help to support. These are shared responsibilities; if every group assumes its share, it assures Al-Anon's everwidening influence.

## TRADITION EIGHT

*Al-Anon Twelfth-Step work should remain forever non-professional, but our service centers may employ special workers.*

This Tradition reasserts the *voluntary* character of Al-Anon's work. We help ourselves through helping others who find themselves troubled by problems like ours. We express our gratitude for Al-Anon's program, and the friendship and understanding of our fellow members, by being ever ready to help another in need.

It is obvious that this special kind of help, this sharing of experience and consolation, cannot be done professionally.

It is true that counseling services by professionals are often needed in special situations. Social service workers, doctors and clergymen who understand the problems created by alcoholism often bring great compassion to this work.

In Al-Anon, which is wholly nonprofessional, there is personal involvement between people who share the same problems. This is the secret of Al-Anon's extraordinary record of success with the families of alcoholics.

Our Service Centers, which spread the Al-Anon message throughout an area, a state, a country or the world, do, of course, require regular office personnel. Yet even in these situations, those who come in contact with people seeking help, by telephone, letter or in person, are invariably Al-Anon members with long experience with alcoholic problems. As staff members they are paid, but this is remuneration for the office work they do, and not for the tireless and devoted personal service which they give as Al-Anon members.

### TRADITION NINE

*Our groups, as such, ought never be organized; but we may create service boards or committees directly responsible to those they serve.*

We speak of Al-Anon as a fellowship or society, indicating that each member is equal to every other. It is not an organization, for that would mean that one or more individuals, or committees, boards or executives, would have the authority to make rules and enforce them. There is no such thing in Al-Anon.

In order to have the fellowship function effectively, however, there must be assignment of responsibility for certain necessary services. The group has a chairman who opens the meetings, a program chairman who plans them, a secretary who keeps the group informed of matters of interest, and handles correspondence, a treasurer who takes care of the funds, and a Group Representative who carries the wishes and ideas of the group to the Area Assembly and brings back to the group information which the Delegate has obtained from the annual World Service Conference. All these functions are services to the members; these are rotating offices, open to the members in turn.

An Information Service (Intergroup) provides a means of communication, in a given locality, between groups and individuals who ask for help. WSO is the heart of Al-Anon through which information and problems clear, from and to groups all over the world. WSO committees and boards deal with the various facets of work—policy, public information, archives, Alateen literature, institutions, and the coordination of translations into other languages.

Every person who has a function in Al-Anon serves, but does not govern. Al-Anon works with an absolute minimum of the services required to hold us together as a united and growing world fellowship.

## TRADITION TEN

*The Al-Anon Family Groups have no opinion on outside issues; hence our name ought never be drawn into public controversy.*

This is an extension of Tradition Six, warning us against involvement, as a group, in any cause or organization outside Al-Anon. As individuals we are free to engage in any activities that interest us, so long as we do not in any way involve Al-Anon.

Our many thousands of members are people of widely different ways of life, of various races, creeds and colors, with political affiliations that vary with party, social status and country.

If a group were to take sides on any issue, however worthy the cause, it would lead to dissension and division within our ranks.

This Tradition is a precaution against any activities that might divert us from our primary purpose, which is to help the families and friends of alcoholics.

## TRADITION ELEVEN

*Our public relations policy is based on attraction rather than promotion; we need always maintain personal anonymity at the level of press, radio, TV and films. We need guard with special care the anonymity of all AA members.*

The acceptance and good will which Al-Anon enjoy has grown out of public recognition of the effectiveness of our program. This has proved the wisdom of allowing our fellowship to grow on a solid foundation of achievement, rather than to promote through extravagant promises and dramatizing of our work. It is results alone that speak for Al-Anon. Those who have found comfort, enlightenment and a richer life are its best salesmen. The attraction of this fellowship, on its merits, is powerful and unfailing; we rely on this to spread its beneficent influence.

Personal anonymity is part of this attraction. It assures those who seek us out that their privacy will be guarded by every member.

Al-Anon has a special responsibility in relation to the anonymity of AA members. Many alcoholics, particularly when they are newcomers to AA, still feel that their alcoholism is a stigma. Often there are practical social and business reasons why they do not wish their affiliation with AA known to others. Everyone in Al-Anon is therefore bound to protect the anonymity of all members of both AA and Al-Anon.

This applies equally to communications between individuals and to public media. Telling the Al-Anon story by means of newspapers, television, or radio should always be done without revealing the identity of individuals.

## TRADITION TWELVE

*Anonymity is the spiritual foundation of all our Traditions, ever reminding us to place principles above personalities.*

Much of the Al-Anon philosophy is crystallized in this Tradition.

Here the word *anonymity* goes far beyond the simple idea of keeping the identity of members from exposure. It says, in effect, that the principles by which we find our help are of far greater importance than the individual who gives or receives that help. It implies that, no matter who you are. or what your views, attitudes and wishes may be, all this must be subordinated to the spiritual principles established for the greatest good of the greatest number. In this sense, we acknowledge ourselves to be anonymities, for principle is everything. Acceptance of this idea may come slowly to many of us; it requires real humility.

Eventually we learn, with a sense of discovery, that this Tradition has within it the solution to many conflicts that may arise.

As humans, our minds are set in certain opinions and views that grow out of our personal experience. They seem so right to us that it is difficult to give way to an opposing view held by someone else. But when the conflicting ideas are examined in the light of spiritual principles, the right solution will be found.

This Tradition has great inspiration for us as individuals. Those who learn to remind themselves always to place principles above personalities have found that many a problem solves itself.

CHAPTER X

# APPLICATION OF THE TWELVE TRADITIONS TO GROUP PROBLEMS

When an Al-Anon group is formed, there is tacit agreement among the members that they will abide by the teachings of the fellowship. Those teachings, as they apply to the individual, are stated in the Twelve Steps; for the unity of the groups, in the Twelve Traditions.

The Traditions are guides based on hard-won experience with group problems. They have served AA well; they serve Al-Anon equally well where there is willingness to learn what the Traditions mean, and how to apply them. They give unfailing assurance of the survival and growth of the group.

When three or four of us come together, we bring with us heartache, anxiety, shame, fear and confusion. We join forces in an Al-Anon group to help free ourselves from the problem that is depriving us of life, liberty and happiness.

Study of the Twelve Traditions often reduces group problems to manageable size and points to logical, acceptable solutions. Many groups are able to find answers in the Digest of Al-Anon Policies, a booklet containing guides and statements which have grown out of interpretations of the Twelve Traditions and our Twelve Concepts of Service.

The Al-Anon World Service Office (WSO) receives letters each year from bewildered members who have encountered baffling group problems. Often they write in a desperate attempt to save a group that seems doomed to failure, sometimes because of the willfulness of a single member.

Each of these letters is answered, and the answers are always based on one or more of the Twelve Traditions which Al-Anon adapted to its own needs from Alcoholics Anonymous.

### Obedience to the Unenforceable

We speak of the Traditions as guides. They are only that. They are not laws, rules, regulations or any other sort of compulsion. To those who are familiar with business or government, such lack of management control may be unthinkable.

What, then, holds the Al-Anon fellowship together? What makes it grow and show such astounding results?

It is based on a set of principles which its members use in solving problems related to alcoholism. Al-Anon derives its strength from *concentrating those principles on that one problem*. It holds together by means of a loving understanding among its members. Al-Anon is united—without organization, without management, without a chain of command or a set of rules—by its members' willingness *to be obedient to the unenforceable*.

Willingly they struggle to face up to their personal problems and solve them with the help of the Twelve Steps of spiritual re-motivation. Willingly they apply the Twelve Traditions to the affairs of the groups. Nobody compels them. They are learning to overcome self-will, false pride, resentment and self-pity by recognizing that principles are more important than personalities and by accepting a program on which they know they can depend for help.

## Solving Group Problems

These examples come from actual group experiences. In each instance the solution of the problem is found in one or more of the Traditions.

### a.

The wife of a member of AA told, at an Al-Anon meeting, some of her husband's drinking episodes. What she said at the meeting was repeated by another member. Within days, this irresponsible gossiping came to the ears of the AA husband, led to a bitter falling out with his Al-Anon wife, caused dissension in the group, and ended by the husband's return to the bottle, with what he considered a good excuse.

In reading Tradition Eleven we are encouraged to guard the anonymity of both Al-Anon and AA members. What is said at an Al-Anon meeting is said with the implicit promise that no word goes beyond the meeting room.

This means we agree not to repeat anything said at a meeting, not even by referring to it in casual conversation *where it may seem to be quite harmless.*

### b.

"At our meetings we try to let each person around the table have a minute or so to talk on the subject of the meeting. But as soon as it gets around to one certain member, he gives a blow-by-blow description of all he has suffered from his wife's drinking. It always ends by his using up all the rest of the meeting time."

Our First Tradition says: "Our *common welfare* should come first." If one member monopolizes the time and attention of the group, the meeting is not serving the others. Some of those present are deprived of an opportunity to speak. Someone's helpful message may be lost. We must consider the welfare of the entire group. It does not even help the obsessive complainer to air his woes at such length. Perhaps more listening would give him some answers to his problem.

The Chairman can interrupt courteously and ask the next person to make some comments on the subject of the meeting, and can also emphasize, at the beginning of these round-the-table sessions, that each person has but one or two minutes to speak in order to give everyone an equal opportunity.

**c.**

"Several members of our group seem more interested in planning social get-togethers like parties and picnics than in talking about Al-Anon. They resent it when some of the others remind them what we come to Al-Anon for...."

According to Tradition Three, we are gathered together for mutual aid as *families of alcoholics*. Again, Tradition One says: "personal progress depends on unity."

Al-Anon has unlimited possibilities *for helping us solve problems associated with alcoholism*, but when we go beyond that, we are not fulfilling our purpose. When two factions are disagreed on a situation like this, it is heading for disunity. We come to Al-Anon for help and solutions, and not for amusement. Individuals in the group may share social occasions; this has nothing to do with Al-Anon other than as a pleasant fringe benefit!

**d.**

"Is it permissible for the alcoholic wife of an AA member to attend Al-Anon meetings?"

Tradition Five says our purpose is to help families of alcoholics. Because we make our meetings available to all who feel they are, or have been affected by someone else's drinking, many meetings are attended by recovering alcoholics. They are welcome and in addition to their own program, they may use Al-Anon to focus on family recovery.

### e.

"Several members of our group invariably decline to voice their thoughts and experiences at meetings. They say they are too shy—they'd rather listen to the others."

If we follow our First Tradition which reads: "Our common welfare should come first," it means that every Al-Anon member should use the privilege of helping the others in the group by participating.

One member wrote: "Remember, speaking is sharing your thoughts, your hopes, your strength and your weakness—it is the beginning of growth within you. You may just possess the key to someone's closed mind or heart. It is in giving that we receive. Only those who have shared their experiences with a problem can truly understand each other. If everyone would rather listen than speak, we would not have the active Al-Anon meetings we do, nor the books, nor the literature. All this is here today because so many have been unselfish."

### f.

"Our group has always held its meetings in the evening. Recently some of the newer members suggested changing to a day-time hour. This is not convenient for the majority. Shouldn't the others go along with those of us who want to continue to meet in the evening?"

Many members with young children find it difficult to attend meetings in the evening, when their youngsters need care and they can't afford baby sitters. Often it is impossible for them to attend Al-Anon meetings at all, particularly when active alcoholism in the home prevents them from leaving the children with someone who cannot be responsible for them. This leaves many free only during the hours when their children are in school.

Shouldn't their welfare be considered too, under our First Tradition?

The obvious solution is to suggest that those who want to meet in the daytime start another group, which they can then build up with others in a similar situation.

This might be an opportunity for the existing group to put Al-Anon's philosophy of love into practice. They can help the new group get started and encourage them in every way to make it successful, by explaining Al-Anon procedures, providing some Conference-Approved Literature, and visiting the new group whenever possible. Under such conditions, what appears to be separation is really promoting Al-Anon unity.

### g.

"The Chairman of our group—she calls it MY group—permits no opposition to her ideas. Many newcomers drop off after one or two visits, although they need Al-Anon very much. She says it's because they're 'not ready'."

From our monthly publication, The *FORUM:*

"A good Al-Anon group is the sum total of its members and not the property of a founder or a self-important Mr. or Mrs. Al-Anon."

According to our Second Tradition, no person in a group, Information Service (Intergroup) or at the World Service Office, has authority to control or direct. An individual who assumes such authority should be set straight on the *equality* of all members of Al-Anon. An experienced, understanding older member of the group might speak to the offender privately and suggest that she allow leadership to rotate among the others in the group. Since such a personality is often difficult to persuade, stronger measures may have to be taken, perhaps ultimately to ask her to leave the group. Her desire to direct may stem from the best of motives, so anything that is said, or any action that is taken, should be motivated by patience, love and understanding.

In some instances the members of such a group have left it and re-formed without her. This course may be necessary if it cannot be handled in any other way, but it is, in a sense, running away from a problem that, with tact and kindness, could be solved without depriving the offending member of the benefits of Al-Anon membership.

### h.

"We are enclosing a flyer describing what is termed an Al-Anon Retreat, to be held at one of our local churches. Although it is the faith to which I belong, along with most of the members of our group, I have objected to this identification of Al-Anon with a specific church. Please help."

Traditionally, Al-Anon does not sponsor such gatherings, worthy and helpful though they may be. There can be no such thing as an Al-Anon Retreat, any more than there is an Al-Anon hospital, rest home or clinic.

According to Tradition Three, we may call ourselves an Al-Anon group provided that, as a group, we have *no other affiliation.* Tradition Six says we ought never to endorse, finance or *lend our name to any outside enterprise,* lest we be diverted from our primary spiritual aim.

The Al-Anon name cannot properly be used to identify or publicize retreats or any other activities sponsored by others. Even when most or all of the participants consider themselves members of Al-Anon, we should avoid anything that might cause public misunderstanding of our purpose or function.

Experience has shown that no reference should be made to the participation of Al-Anon members in advance notices or reports. Even if an entire group wishes to attend the retreat, they do so as individuals, not as Al-Anon members.

**i.**

"We have a problem which is going to be the ruination of our group which has been such a success in the past. One male member repeats everything we say at meetings to his AA wife, who then repeats them to the members of her AA group, many of whom are our husbands. Often the stories are so distorted and exaggerated as to be unrecognizable, which just makes it worse. This has led to a great deal of family dissension and several slips. We have had several serious talks with this member but he just laughs it off. What can we do?"

If he is not responsive to your requests that he observe discretion about what goes on at your meetings, it might help to plan a meeting built on Tradition Five: "Each Al-Anon group has but one purpose: to help families of alcoholics. We do this by practicing the Twelve Steps of AA ourselves, by encouraging and understanding our alcoholic relatives and by welcoming and giving comfort to families of alcoholics."

If even a single member causes difficulties for the families of alcoholics, your group cannot fully serve its purpose. Gossip destroys the very thing we join forces to achieve—serenity, acceptance and growth.

Meetings can be planned where each participant is assigned one angle of the problem for discussion. Members can speak frankly about what can happen in a family as a result of such careless gossip.

Some groups have an older member explain in private to the offending member that he may be impeding his own recovery by his unguarded talk.

If all this fails, for the "greatest good of the greatest number," he may have to be warned and asked to leave the group if he continues to ignore the spiritual counsel of the Fifth Tradition.

### j.

"A friend of one of our members, a wealthy and generous woman who has long been interested in alcoholism as a social problem, has offered us a gift of one thousand dollars. She is convinced that we can attract many more members through newspaper announcements and widespread distribution of our literature, and that such a gift, in Al-Anon's hands, would do a great deal of good. How can we refuse without offending her?"

The Seventh Tradition simply states that we should be fully self-supporting and decline outside contributions. There are excellent reasons for this.

Perhaps she might not be hurt if it was explained that our growth must come from within. Al-Anon members should not be deprived of the privilege of supporting their own fellowship. Even the difficulties we face, and they are many, are wholesome disciplines.

Early experience of both AA and Al-Anon has been the guide in establishing this Tradition. Although this generous donor would surely not attempt to influence or control, we would, by accepting her gift, set a precedent that might mean selling our independence. Other individuals and organizations who might want to use the united influence of Al-Anon could try to establish their right by making substantial contributions.

Our groups need only enough money to defray expenses for rent, literature, refreshments and contributions to the WSO and the Area World Service Assembly. Every group should be able to take care of these modest obligations.

Funds needed by an Information Service (intergroup) should come from the groups concerned. They are responsible for its support, just as it is responsible for providing service and liaison between prospective members and the groups.

If the Al-Anon WSO were to accept contributions from outsiders—and they are occasionally offered—it would change the entire structure of the fellowship. It would affect the close relationship between the WSO and the groups.

It is an abiding condition of the Al-Anon fellowship that its members support their groups and the groups support the WSO, which uses these funds to provide world-wide service. This interdependence is a wholesome and sustaining condition, preserving all Al-Anon in unity and equality.

### k.

A member of a group, deeply interested in civil rights, tries to persuade the other members to take part in demonstrations.

There are many worthy causes of interest to some or all of the members of a group. But our only concern, as Al-Anon members, is to help ourselves and others to live with the problem of alcoholism.

Tradition Ten states that the Al-Anon Family Groups take no stand on outside issues.

Individually we are free to do anything we wish to about other causes and organizations, but not as an Al-Anon group.

A member of another group, interested in a foundling home, feels that the group should help a cause so worthy. And there is a certain elementary logic in her position: as human beings, striving to better ourselves and the world, we are moved and concerned for the welfare of others. But if Al-Anon were to involve itself in every worthwhile cause, where could we draw the line that would keep our fellowship intact to do its job?

The Traditions wisely suggest that Al-Anon groups devote themselves to Al-Anon's purposes.

**I.**

"We have a member who is separated from her alcoholic husband and has the care of four small children. We know she is having a hard time getting along; several of us have given her money from time to time. At our last business meeting someone brought up the question of helping her by giving her a few dollars from the group contributions each week. Some of us do not agree that this should be done. What's the answer?"

What would the answer be if there were more members in equal need? Could the group afford to help them all and still fulfill its primary purpose, which it does by supporting the expense of meeting, and by providing literature for those who need emotional and spiritual help?

Distress cases occur fairly frequently in Al-Anon groups; once a group has helped a needy family, it has established a precedent. How can it then refuse to help others in need? It is not the responsibility of the group to act as a welfare oreganization; many social agencies are equipped and financed for this.

Tradition Five describes the purposes of Al-Anon: to help families of alcoholics by practicing the Twelve Steps of AA ourselves, by encouraging and understanding our alcoholic relatives and by welcoming and giving comfort to families of alcoholics. This does not include giving financial aid *as a group.*

Individuals who wish to give or lend money to others may, of course, do so, but funds contributed to the group should be used only for group obligations.

**m.**

Questions frequently arise that call for clarification of the relationship of Al-Anon to AA.

1. Should AA literature be displayed at Al-Anon meetings?

2. Should some groups which meet in the same building as an AA group and get together with them afterward provide the refreshments for these occasions?

3. Should Al-Anon groups provide funds for starting an AA group, paying rent, providing refreshments and even buying a stock of literature?

Tradition Six says in part: "we ought never to finance any outside enterprise" and concludes with "although a separate entity we should always cooperate with AA."

1) AA literature is readily available at an AA meeting. Neither fellowship makes it a practice to stock or distribute the other's literature.

2) If the Al-Anon group regularly pays for joint refreshments, it is financing AA's share of this obligation unless, of course, it is Al-Anon's way of paying rent for a meeting room. The funds contributed to AA are used to defray AA expenses; those that are contributed to Al-Anon are used for Al-Anon purposes.

3) Finally, for an Al-Anon group to help an AA group get started is definitely an intrusion into the affairs of a separate fellowship which is covered in Tradition Six. Close as we are to AA—we do not take over AA's responsibilities or activities. AA is just as dedicated to solving the problems of the alcoholic as we are to solving those of the alcoholic's family; our two functions should remain separate.

In all our relations with AA we should be guided not by rigid rules, but by common sense. Where finances are concerned, most Al-Anon groups have all they can do to meet their own obligations with the funds contributed at their meetings. Financial involvements on either side can create awkward situations.

There have been many instances when AA has helped a struggling Al-Anon group, but every effort should be made to become and remain self-supporting.

### n.

A group in need of more funds than are provided by its regular contributions asks whether the idea of a public raffle would be acceptable.

Two of the Traditions question this idea.

Tradition Seven says that every group ought to be fully self-supporting. If this raffle yields a profit, as it is intended to do, we are accepting help from others for the support of Al-Anon.

Tradition Eleven concerns anonymity at the level of press, radio, TV and films. But most AA newcomers and many AA and Al-Anon groups take their anonymity much further. Therefore it would be inconsiderate for Al-Anon members to engage in such an enterprise.

The proposed raffle could, of course, be undertaken if only Al-Anon and AA members were involved.

### o.

A State Alcohol Committee has enlisted the aid of various local organizations in helping alcoholics and their families. One of these is the local Al-Anon group, which agreed to cooperate, and undertook to pay part of the cost of circularizing a mailing list.

This activity is questionable on the basis of a number of Al-Anon Traditions.

First, Al-Anon would appear to the public to have affiliated itself with the local Committee on Alcoholism. Our Third Tradition states that we may call ourselves an Al-Anon group "provided that, as a group, we have no other affiliation."

Second, Tradition Six states that "we ought never to endorse nor lend our name to any outside enterprise, lest problems of money, property or prestige divert us from our primary spiritual aim." The letter gives the impression that the Alcoholism Committee considers Al-Anon merely a branch of AA or the sponsoring Committee or both. Al-Anon is not under the sponsorship of any Committee.

Third, it also puts the Al-Anon group under obligation to support the Committee's activities whether or not they conform to Al-Anon ideas and standards.

Such a concerted effort may make it possible to reach many more people than Al-Anon could by itself. Breaking Traditions, however, may result in accomplishing immediate good at the cost of lessening Al-Anon's future usefulness by submerging its identity or diverting it from its purpose.

**p.**

From time to time a group may question certain activities of another group which it feels is violating our Eleventh Tradition: "Our public relations policy is based on attraction rather than promotion." Among the practices to which objection has been voiced are the following:

1. Announcing in a newspaper the formation of an Al-Anon group, or publishing the time and place of a group's meeting.

2. Mention of the Al-Anon fellowship on TV or radio, even when no names are given and no persons can be identified.

3. Working with "outsiders"—clergymen, doctors and social workers—to interest them in Al-Anon as a source of help for families who consult them about problems connected with alcoholism.

4. The use of a conspicuous book jacket on an Al-Anon book.

These objections may be due to misunderstanding of several of the Traditions. The Fifth states: "Each Al-Anon group has but one purpose: to help families of alcoholics." This Tradition ends with the words: "by welcoming and giving comfort to families of alcoholics."

We welcome and help by making it known that there is such a fellowhsip as Al-Anon. Whatever we can do *that does not violate the anonymity of an individual* is permissible, provided, of course, that it is kept on a serious and dignified level.

We try to reach as many of these troubled families as we can. Our Twelfth-Step work is not limited to those who have been fortunate enough to hear about Al-Anon accidentally. We have a message to carry.

When our Eleventh Tradition says: "Our public relations policy is based on attraction rather than promotion" it suggests we should not hesitate to attract to it anyone who needs the help of Al-Anon.

There are many acceptable ways of attracting people to Al-Anon without promotion. We can feel perfectly free to inform others who work in the field of alcoholism about Al-Anon. These include individual professionals who are consulted by people in trouble, as well as state, provincial and local councils and associations working with alcoholism problems, churches, hospitals, and, of course, AA.

### q.

"The AA group in our neighborhood is favorable to Al-Anon and has encouraged the spouses of its members to start a group. We hesitate because we feel we cannot afford the initial expense, and rent, refreshments and literature. The AA group has offered to provide the money to start with. Shall we accept it?"

It is traditional, in both AA and Al-Anon, not to enter into financial involvements, whether to accept or give help. According to Tradition Seven, every group should be fully self-supporting. On that basis it would not be desirable to accept the generous offer made by the AA group. There are two alternatives:

If the prospective members cannot start out with enough money to cover one month's rent and a small stock of literature, funds to cover these expenses might be borrowed from a member or members, with the understanding that it will be repaid as promptly as possible.

It might be better for the group at first to limit its expenditure for literature to the minimum. When the group is financially able, it can spread its wings a little, pay for a meeting place, order a more adequate stock of literature and set some money aside for its contributions to WSO and the Area Assembly.

The offer of the AA group has a greater significance than the merely financial; such whole-hearted interest could mean an early and substantial membership for the new group which would enable it to stand on its own feet.

### r.

"One of our members is acquainted with the author of an inspirational book which has had some acceptance. She would like to invite this author to give a talk at one of our meetings and to autograph copies of her book of which she would bring along a number of copies to sell. Some of us are opposed to this because the book is not directly connected with Al-Anon or alcoholism.

While it is certainly in order to invite outsiders to speak at an Al-Anon meeting occasionally, it should be someone who is familiar with the problems of the families of alcoholics. That is Al-Anon's primary concern.

This situation, as the member describes it, involves Tradition Six which says we ought never to endorse, finance or lend our name to any outside enterprise. This we would be doing in having the book offered for sale at an Al-Anon meeting.

**s.**

"We are a metropolitan group consisting largely of successful career women. Whatever problems we have, shortage of funds is not among them.

"One faction is very much interested in engaging the services of a psychiatric counselor who would attend our meetings and help advise us on our problems. The opposing faction feels that this does not fit into the Al-Anon program.

"We need impartial advice."

The answer comes, of course, directly from our Traditions. "Our Twelfth-Step work should remain forever non-professional, although our service centers may employ special workers."

The task proposed for the counselor would essentially be Twelfth-Step work which, in Al-Anon, is performed by members who share and understand the problems that plague those whose lives are disturbed by compulsive drinking. The exception mentioned in the Eighth Tradition refers only to office workers who take care of the business of the service centers.

Professional and personal advice is not part of the Al-Anon program. Members desiring such advice may seek it elsewhere, but not at an Al-Anon meeting.

\* \* \*

Situations and questions such as these are bound to occur wherever people work together. These examples show how the Traditions can be applied to solving problems. They also show that tolerance and common sense are helpful in interpreting them to fit each occasion.

There are times when a group may not be able to find answers to questions they feel are not covered in the service literature: The Digest of Al-Anon and Alateen Policies, The World Service Handbook, The Twelve Concepts of Service, and/or The Al-Anon and Alateen Groups at Work. While many solutions can be found in taking the problem to a District meeting, the Area Committee or the Area Assembly, those problems which are referred to the WSO are brought to the attention of the appropriate committee and staff member familiar with the experiences of other groups which have faced similar difficulties.

# CHAPTER XI

# THE SLOGANS OF AL-ANON

Slogans which have become traditional in AA have been gratefully adopted by most Al-Anon groups. Their recall and interpretation often makes the basis of worthwhile discussions at Al-Anon meetings. In addition, they are helpful in dealing with our day-to-day personal problems.

> First Things First
> Easy Does It
> Live and Let Live
> But For the Grace of God
> Keep an Open Mind
> Let Go and Let God
> Just For Today

## *First Things First*

Sometimes in our enthusiasm to get things going in this new way of life we don't know where to begin. There are so many things that need to be done, so many areas to tackle. If we just sit down and think out which is the first and most important thing, the less important ones usually fall into place. If, for instance, we can see that our own integrity is the most important thing, our alcoholic's sobriety and the family's welfare are likely to follow as a result. What might appear a selfish attitude is discovered to be the first and the most important thing, benefiting others as well as ourselves.

### Easy Does It

We Al-Anon members often expect too much too soon. We expect too much fo the alcoholics after they have joined AA, and of ourselves. So easy does it. Take it a day at a time. Living the AA and Al-Anon program is a lifetime job. Making a start with sincerity and steady progress is what counts. Pushing ourselves or the alcoholic leads to frustrations and tensions. These are the things we want to avoid, and we can learn to do this by remembering that Easy Does It.

### Live and Let Live

Along with the release of tension, Al-Anon brings us to a more reasonable attitude toward trying to manage other people's lives. We come to believe that *our* way to a more serene outlook may not be the solution for the alcoholic, our relatives and friends, or other members of Al-Anon.. We try to improve ourselves rather than to look for faults in others.

### But For the Grace of God

No matter how deeply scientists may analyze, there is always an "X" factor which they cannot explain. The grace of God is indeed behind the miracles of recovery in Al-Anon. The more we open our hearts to it the greater and more satisfying will be the recovery.

### Keep an Open Mind

We can set aside any prejudices or doubts we may have about what Al-Anon can do for us. We try not to judge the group or the program by one or two meetings. Sooner or later a member will say something that reaches our heart as well as our mind. We keep an open mind about alcoholism as a disease by learning all we can about it. We go to as many open AA meetings as possible; they will clear a mental pathway for new concepts about all alcoholics, and especially ours. We try to keep an open mind about the Twelve Steps; they can fill us with hope and serenity.

## Let Go and Let God

This can be a guide to better living. When we turn our wills and our lives over to the care of God, we get rid of conflicts within ourselves created through being self-centered.

After taking our moral inventory, we can have a desire to be different. When we admit this to God, we will find it easier to allow His wisdom to guide us. As we begin to change, our faith grows. As our faith grows our fears and tensions will go.

Every day we have decisions to make and problems to overcome. If we supply the willingness, God supplies the power. Through this way of living we grow spiritually. At the end of each day we realize we have found serenity through letting go and letting God.

## Just For Today

This slogan is usually developed by the anonymous statements which follow:

*"Just for today* I will try to live through this day only, and not tackle my whole life problem at once. I can do something for twelve hours that would appall me if I felt I had to keep it up for a lifetime.

*"Just for today* I will be happy. Abraham Lincoln said, "Most folks are as happy as they make up their minds to be."

"*Just for today* I will adjust myself to what is, and not try to adjust everything to my own desires. I will take my "luck" as it comes and fit myself to it.

"*Just for today* I will try to strengthen my mind. I will study, I will learn something useful. I will read something that requires effort, thought and concentration.

"*Just for today* I will exercise my soul in three ways: I will do somebody a good turn, and not get found out; if anybody knows of it, it will not count. I will do at least two things I don't want to do—just for exercise. I will not show anyone that my feelings are hurt; they may be hurt, but today I will not show it.

"*Just for today* I will be agreeable. I will look as well as I can, dress becomingly, keep my voice low, act courteously, refrain from criticizing and fault-finding. I will not try to improve or regulate anybody but myself.

"*Just for today* I will have a program. I may not follow it exactly, but I will have it. This will save me from two pests: hurry and indecision.

"*Just for today* I will have a quiet half hour all by myself, and relax. Some time during this half hour, I will try to get a better perspective of my life.

"*Just for today* I will be unafraid. Especially I will not be afraid to enjoy what is beautiful, and to believe that as I give to the world, so the world will give to me."

# Chapter XII

# THEY FOUND ANSWERS

Personal stories are sometimes more helpful than explanations of Al-Anon. Perhaps you will find in the following pages a story similar to your own. Varieties of experience are included. Stories about wives whose husbands are still drinking; stories about wives with sober partners in AA, husbands who are working the program with their alcoholic wives, and the trials and triumphs of parents and children of alcoholics.

## Stories of Wives

### An Adventure in Growth

By Lois, Wife of the Co-founder of Alcoholics Anonymous.

Bill started drinking a short time before we were married in 1918. He was an alcoholic from the beginning, and so he got drunk every time he drank. I was greatly concerned, but I felt our life together would be so complete that soon he would not need this artificial stimulus. But his drinking grew worse as time went on. We had no children, and my one purpose in life was to help him get over this terrible habit.

Aside from his drinking, we were very happy. We liked the outdoors and took many different kinds of trips together, sometimes hiking with packs on our backs, sometimes traveling by a car so arranged that we could sleep in it. When Bill became interested in the stock market and wanted to investigate certain industries down south, we spent a whole year motorcycling from one plant to another, camping in our tent. I was very grateful for this opportunity to get him away from the city and his constant drinking.

We must have been a funny-looking outfit. Our duffle was packed in waterproof boxes and bundles, hitched on here and there to the machine. Bill didn't care particularly about driving, and he used to sit in the bathtub or side-car and think, his long legs hanging over the prow; while I, a little peanut by comparison, drove.

Later when Bill's alcoholism became very bad, I still arranged many weekends in the open, thus for him there was a reversal of the usual alcoholic's pattern of weekend drinking. He rested up on Saturday and Sunday from his week's work of drinking.

Finally, when drinking became practically constant, he himself realized he must do something about it. Together we tried everything we could think of. He set up one kind of control plan after another: never to drink alone, to drink only before meals, never to have liquor in the house, to drink only at home with me. He read psychological books, consulted doctors, and went to sanitariums. Twice I gave up my job and we escaped for three months to the country for renewal and rebuilding. Nothing worked. I'd had to assume all family responsibilities and make all decisions. It was tragic indeed to see such a fine man so completely beaten and hopeless.

By now we lived entirely to ourselves. We had dropped all our friends or had been dropped by them; we saw as little as possible of our families. Our whole life had simmered down to one terrible fight against alcohol.

Then in 1934 an old friend appeared at our home, bright-eyed and sober, although previously he had been considered a hopeless drunkard. He came to tell Bill about his release from alcoholism. Soon afterward Bill went to the hospital to get the liquor out of his system so he could think out clearly what had happened to his friend. While in the hospital, Bill had such a deeply moving spiritual experience that he came home a completely changed man. He received a release from alcoholism that has lasted to this day.

We were joyful, grateful and awestruck by this miracle, and neither of us doubted that Bill's freedom from alcohol was complete and final. He worked tirelessly trying to "sober up all the drunks in the world." At least half of these, it seemed to me, in all stages of recovery and non-recovery, filled our house continually. Since there was as yet no AA, we attended meetings of the spiritual group to which our helpful friend belonged.

After a while I began to wonder why I was not as happy as I should be. This wonderful thing for which I had worked all my married life had really happened. Bill was sober, ready and willing to resume a husband's normal responsibilities. And yet I continued to nag and direct, not realizing how important it was for him to assume his responsibilities.

I resented the fact that Bill and I had no life together any more. I was left alone while he was off somewhere scouting up new drunks and working on old ones. My life's job of sobering up Bill, which had made me feel so needed, suddenly had vanished, and I had not yet found anything to fill the void. There was also the feeling of being on the outside of a tight little clique of alcoholics, where no mere wife could enter. I did not fully understand what was going on within myself until one Sunday Bill asked me if I was ready to go to a meeting with him. To my own surprise as well as his, I burst forth with "Damn your old meeting!'' and threw a shoe as hard as I could.

This display of temper woke me up to the fact that I had been wallowing in self-pity. In the light of this awakening I could see not only that Bill's feverish activity with alcoholics was absolutely necessary to his sobriety but also that he really was developing spiritually. I saw too that if I did not want to be left behind I had better join the procession and strive for more spiritual growth myself.

As the years went on Bill and I were concerned to find that strained relations, such as ours had been, often developed in families after the first starry-eyed period of AA was over. We were heartsick and puzzled to realize that although many alcoholics were recovering through this wonderful new way of life, their home lives were sometimes far from serene. We began to learn how many adjustments had to be made and how much the partner of the alcoholic needed the program also. I was just as powerless over my husband's alcoholism as he was, since I failed in every attempt to control his drinking. I tried to manage Bill's life, although not able to manage my own. I wanted to get inside his brain and turn the screws in what I thought was the right direction.

Because my thinking was distorted and my nerves overwrought, I held fears and attitudes that certainly were not sane. Having been told over and over by friends how patient, longsuffering and good I was to assume the roles of mother, nurse, guardian and breadwinner, I began to develop a smug feeling of righteousness. At the same time, illogically, I felt a failure at my life's job of helping Bill to sobriety. All this had made me blind to the fact that I, too, needed to turn my will and my life over to the care of God. Smugness is the very worst sin of all, I believe. No shaft of light can pierce the armor of self-righteousness.

When I was able to see through this smugness even a little, I knew that I resented the interference of certain persons and that I had been short and irritable with them, thus imperiling long-standing friendships. I remember that on one nerve-wracking day, I threw a book at a friend who was trying to help me. Throwing seems to have been my pet temper outlet.

When I began to work at being really honest, I discovered that many of the things I thought I did unselfishly were pure rationalizations, tricks to get my own way about something. Admitting my wrongs helped to change Bill's and my "mother-and-bad-boy" relationship and to bring it closer to the ideal of partnership in marriage.

I was deeply hurt because someone else had done in a few minutes what I had tried to do unsuccessfully throughout my whole married life. Now I have learned that a wife can rarely, if ever, do this job. The sick alcoholic feels his wife's account has been written on the credit side of life's ledger, while his own has been on the debit side. Therefore he believes she cannot possibly understand. Another alcoholic, with a similar debit entry, immediately identifies himself as no non-alcoholic can. I found no peace of mind until I recognized this important fact.

While striving for humility myself, it was inspiring to see my husband's growth in the same direction. It is natural for alcoholics to rebound from inferiority to superiority when they first join AA. They feel low, lost, and alone while drinking, but in AA they suddenly find they belong to the most wonderful group of people in the whole world, people who understand and who are striving to live by the highest principles. But as the newcomer works on the program, this superiority phase disappears, and he begins really to grow in humility.

When I worked at cleaning away the debris of the past by

making amends for harms done, I was building a bulwark against hard knocks that might come along later. Even more important, I was gaining new serenity and joy in living.

I am beginning to understand how to pray. Bargaining with God is not real prayer and asking Him for what I want, even good things, is not the highest form of prayer. I used to think I knew what was good for me when I, the captain, would give my instructions to my lieutenant, God, to carry out.

I have set aside a little while night and morning for meditation, and gratitude is one of my principal subjects, gratitude for all the love, the beauty, and the friends around me, gratitude even for the hard days that taught me so much. Thus I have made a start toward improving my conscious contact with God.

I know I need to continue my efforts toward growth. One either moves forward or slides backward. Nothing has done more to urge me forward than the need to carry the AA message to the families of alcoholics who are seeking a way out of their dilemma. The helping of others over the hard path that one has trod strengthens both travelers, the helper and the helped.

AA often speaks of the Twelve Steps as tools. An extension of this idea came to me the other day. There is a striking analogy between working on ourselves in AA or in Al-Anon and cultivating a garden.

Our inheritance and early environment compose the soil out of which grow our thoughts and actions, both flowers and weeds. To raise flowers we must get rid of the weeds.

Our garden tools are the knowledge of ourselves and our motives, our honesty in facing ourselves, our desire to help others and our awareness of God. These principles of AA are the tools which we use.

We must keep cultivating with these really effective implements lest our garden be over-run by weeds.

Soils vary; some are rocky, sandy, or swampy; others are more fertile. But whatever the soil, there are appropriate flowers that can be grown. Even the desert blooms.

One gardener may find it difficult to uproot the weeds because his tools are constantly being dulled against the many large rocks in his plot. But by repeated sharpening of his hoe and by careful selection of his plants he may at last be able to grow a charming rock garden.

Another takes it for granted that a beautiful garden will be produced because the soil is rich. Since he does not bother to cultivate well, he may some day wake up to find the garden filled with insidious weeds that thrive in fertile ground, the weeds of smugness and self-righteousness.

In just this way the life of many a self-pitying wife or husband can become choked and unproductive.

The Al-Anon Family Groups show us the need to cultivate the gardens of our lives and how this can be done through the use of AA's Twelve Steps.

### Before ... and Many Years After

Another Al-Anon wife's story.

My husband still carries in his wallet the following letter which I wrote him from Nantucket in 1947. It reminds both of us how much has changed since then. The letter is one I could not have written after I found Al-Anon. But my husband tells me that it is typical of the attitudes held by the wives of many of his AA friends in those unhappy "before" days.

"I hope you are taking care of yourself and going easy on the liquor. I just can't understand a person of your caliber resorting to such furtive drinking as you do. I was hurt after you left when I found empty bottles in the closet behind a suit case. At home I find them all over the house, and it makes me nervous and discouraged. I am fast losing faith in everything and wonder why we had to have children. I would have banked on your strong character and I thought our kids would have something to live up to. Now, when I look at you as you have been for the last year, I feel you aren't the same man I married. I have never felt more lonely.

"You must be pretty unhappy to want to lose yourself this way. If it's me or your job, or the children, do something rather than destroy yourself. I think two or three drinks before dinner are fine, but to go on all evening by yourself swigging out of a bottle in closets is revolting.

"In January of this year you promised you would drink normally or give it up. I said I would do anything to help you if you would only tell me what made you drink. In the spring when you called me from Atlantic City, you couldn't speak intelligibly. I decided then that liquor must mean more to you than the children or I do. They have asked me 'Why does Dad do it?'

"I have to write you this because you won't listen when I try talk to you about it. Yet when we were married you said we should always talk over our problems together, that our marriage would never go on the rocks. I wonder if there is still time to save it. If we go on this way, pretty soon we will end up hating each other and probably the children will hate us too. Try to understand if you can, because I still love the old you very much and always will."

My husband came into AA not because of this letter, and certainly through no help of mine. I was just a zombie walking around without faith in God or in life. Saturated with self-pity, I no longer trusted myself to hope, for fear of new disappointment. I am sure if the "men in the little white coats" had looked into our windows, they would have taken me and not John. At least the things he did were under the influence of alcohol, whereas I, apparently sane, spent my days rehearsing speeches to an imaginary husband.

When John could no longer bear what was happening to himself, he did something about it. The night he came home to announce he had contacted AA started like any other. He had telephoned to say he had missed his train and wouldn't be home for dinner. As usual he missed a few more and when he finally arrived, I was in bed. He said to our eldest daughter, "Get your mother downstairs. I want to talk to her."

Wearily I donned a robe and thought, what is it now? He had "resigned" a few months before from the company he had been with for fifteen years. I allowed myself a vague hope that he had got a new job. He sat in his usual chair not quite as drunk as I expected, and said "I have contacted AA." My answer was "so what?" I went back upstairs to bed.

Although I had heard vaguely of AA, I thought he was beyond their help. Deep down I could sense his despair and knew that he did not mean to break promise after promise. This very fact left me only more bewildered and fearful of his sanity.

For months I had been trying to make a decision to walk out. But I felt like a rat leaving a sinking ship. A few months before he had set his bed on fire, and I worried about what would become of him. And where would I go with three children? After nineteen years of marriage I couldn't envision life without him, yet I was frightened at what his drinking was doing to all of us.

Half-heartedly I went to AA meetings with John. Gradually I began to realize that this was not the happy ending to all our problems but rather a happy beginning of a new way of life for both of us. Learning in AA that alcoholism was a disease lifted a load from my shoulders and removed feelings of guilt and rejection. Through attending Al-Anon I was given the inspiration to apply the Twelve Steps to myself.

My husband had been sober in AA for over five years when our Al-Anon group was formed. Although I had gone to hundreds of AA meetings with John and believed in the Steps as an ideal way of life, I was not gaining the serenity of complete reliance on a Higher Power which I had seen in many AA members. Nor did I find the quality of serenity by talking to the non-alcoholics at AA meetings.

Discussing the Steps with others in Al-Anon whose experience paralleled mine made the whole program come alive to me. Trying to practice these principles in all my affairs has added a new dimension to my life and given me back a faith in God which I thought I had lost forever.

The Twelve Steps are most important to me, and it is only to the degree that I try to live by these principles every day that I see and experience the amount of good they bring. They have made me more receptive to my Higher Power, and I now realize that the grace of God is given to all of us. Whether or not we accept it is our own decision to make.

I use the First Step whenever a big problem confronts me, substituting for the word alcohol the name of my difficulty. This Step brought home to me forcibly that I am powerless over other people. The only person I can really change is myself. I can only try to understand others but I can never really know their inner selves, their temptations and their struggles. My own life was unmanageable so how could I presume to manage another's life?

I had to turn the searchlight of truth on my actions and reactions which had become so unstable. In my case, self-righteousness was a definite barrier toward reaching any Higher Power. I know realize my own inadequacy and I know that I could not pride myself on not having the disease of alcoholism. I owe that to the grace of God.

I found it hard to make the decision to turn my will and my life over to God as I understood Him. For me the opening of that locked door required the key of prayer and meditation. I had to be willing to go all the way to gain the peace this decision offers. As I began to center my life on a Power greater than myself, I realized that at last I was on the road to serenity of mind and heart. The real barriers to spiritual understanding, I think, are within ourselves.

I had so many shortcomings that I found the word humble took on new meaning. It meant patience and honesty to stop rationalizing and to face things realistically. I did not develop all these shortcomings in a day, and lifetime habits are lifetime jobs to correct. Realizing this left me no time to take inventory of my partner, which I think we are all prone to do.

Was I entirely ready to have God remove these defects of character? All I had to do was remind myself just how these defects had robbed me of my peace of mind and led me into unhappy frustrations and wrong thinking. The misery of self-discovery in the Fourth Step can be followed by joy in this complete surrender of putting ourselves in the hands of the only One who can do this for us.

I had been wrong in my attitudes so often that when I became willing to make amends, I was able to clear up misunderstandings and add warmth to friendship by asking forgiveness whenever possible. Apology seems to beget apology, and in this way hurt feelings are mended and the balance of love restored.

As I learn to speak, listen and think with love, I find I can forgive with greater ease. I try to use my own judgment about making amends. Sometimes it can be accomplished better by adopting an understanding and loving attitude than by painful recollections of past mistakes.

I know it is essential for me to establish positive attitudes before I am able to practice the spiritual principles of the Al-Anon program. This helps in keeping my thinking straight and in searching out my motives. We do not realize how negative our thinking is until we make a positive approach to our goals.

Seeking to improve our conscious contact with God through prayer and meditation keeps us receptive to His will for us and the power to carry it out. Constant attendance at Al-Anon meetings helps me to continue growing. Faith does not remain alive automatically in the mind. We are all subject to moods so we must constantly be reminded of what we believe in. I need to seek, through prayer, spiritual reading, church, Al-Anon and AA, for strength to fortify my beliefs.

As I now pray only for knowledge of His will for me, I am reassured by learning many times that what I thought to be disappointments in the past were in reality blessings in disguise.

Nothing mystic or startling such as a spiritual awakening happened to me. But I feel an entirely new attitude of deep gratitude. It is as if my husband and I, in becoming devoted to something greater than ourselves in AA and Al-Anon, have found ourselves and each other.

"Carrying the message" at first brought only frustration to me, because I did not realize in my enthusiasm that the principles of these Twelve Steps must be practiced and firmly believed in before they can be given to others.

It seems to me that just being together at meetings is carrying the message. We are all enriched by the exchange of ideas in Al-Anon. Everyone teaches us something if we but listen with an open mind. Each of us has something to give in this new way of life.

The more I dwell on these principles as I have learned to apply them in Al-Anon the more similarity I find in them to the Sermon on the Mount which, like the Twelve Steps, is a sure guide to serenity and lasting happiness.

## Al-Anon After Sobriety

I heard about the Al-Anon Family Groups about a year after my husband joined AA.

Jack did not seek sobriety of his own volition. In 1943, he was forced to attend a few AA meetings at the insistence of his employer. He did not sober up, he just became wilier at concealment on the job.

Our son at the age of five, suddenly developed a speech difficulty, with no such tendency previously noticeable. When I was questioned by our pediatrician concerning any unusual tensions in the home, I broke down and tearfully confessed that my husband drank too much. At his suggestion, Jack tried psychiatry, though unwillingly. He said *I* was the one who needed treatment. The six months of therapy were expensive and completely ineffectual, because he drank with a vengeance the whole time. There were periods of remission after that, spells of comparative calm and even times of genuine family happiness, but there was always that sword of Damocles casting a shadow over the future.

It is still inconceivable to me that an alcoholic can drink up as much money as mine did. He was a newspaper editor on his way up, with a real flair for subtle humor. In order to help finance the last five years of his drinking, he also wrote fact fiction detective stories at night, fortified by a bottle of whiskey beside him.

Even a sizable inheritance from my father, which I tried to keep intact as a reserve for the uncertain future, went down the drain of alcoholism. But to be truthful, I helped spend some of it. After months of penny pinching, when suddenly faced with yet another batch of drinking tabs to pay, I would rebel and make extravagant purchases that we could ill afford if we were ever to educate our children.

I threatened separation on numerous occasions and Jack retaliated by saying he would skip the state if I went through with it. Once I went so far as to consult a lawyer, but subconsciously I was not ready for separation. For the counselor I chose was a good friend of my husband's who subsequently paid him a handsome fee for campaign stories he wrote which helped him into elective office. This lawyer really did not understand alcoholism. He advised me that in every marriage a little rain must fall. He suggested that sometimes it is the wife's poor housekeeping which causes the friction, that infidelity could be far more disturbing than occasional drunkenness. I still had a home, adequate support and might lose them if we separated. So I gave up the idea and returned home more dispirited and hopeless than ever.

Inevitably, the alcoholism progressed to the point where days off to recover from bouts came closer and closer together. The last six months of his drinking were spent in the basement recreation room. The story I told for the benefit of the children and which I'm sure they did not swallow —was so that he would not disturb my sleep in the morning, as he left at six. In fact, it was the only way he could face a new day—by several drinks from a poorly concealed bottle as soon as he awoke.

I had forgotten how to laugh. I had become a martyr to my home, a perfectionist, withdrawn from any normal social activity, full of self-pity. I now know that my lack of insight into the problem did more to make our children feel insecure and unloved than anything my husband ever did. He was never violent, had a sense of humor that I lacked, and his children loved him, even if they could no longer respect the psychopathic liar he had become. But I wanted their love withheld as revenge for all the suffering he had caused us. So I played on their sympathies and tried my best to alienate them too. I also vented my many frustrations on them—being too permissive at times and unreasonably stern at others. On occasion, I must even have betrayed my unconscious resentment at having borne them, for without them I would not have to endure another day of living with a drunk.

An accepted concept in AA circles is that the alcoholic will not seek treatment until he hits his bottom. However, I hit mine before Jack did. It happened one day in late 1950 when he had been home for two weeks, a zombie in the playroom, going out only to replenish his daily quota of liquor, two quarts by then. He was a bloated, physical wreck; even the doctor's recent warning that he had less than a year to live unless he "moderated" his drinking had no effect. He seemed bent on slow suicide.

The time for concealment was past for me. I went next door to a neighbor to whom I had never breathed a word about our private little hell, and called my husband's boss, the man who had tried to get him to join AA seven years earlier. I told him that Jack did not have the "grippe," that I had decided to separate from him and that if he felt he was still valuable to him as an employee, he could take over. He told me to go home and say nothing about my call. An hour later, he returned it, asking to speak to Jack. He told him he thought he might need different medication—wouldn't it be wise to have the company doctor come over. Jack admitted that maybe he had been hitting it up a little too hard, and before that conversation ended, agreed to speak to two members of AA whom the boss would ask to visit him. A few days later, his two sponsors escorted Jack to Towns Hospital in Manhattan. As he left he warned me that the next time I saw him he'd be in a straitjacket and that sobriety was an impossibility for him. He was sure he was headed for a mental institution for life. This he really believed, and I was almost convinced too. But after ten days in the hospital, he remained sober for seven years until his sudden death of a heart attack in 1958.

It is my firm conviction that had I not been driven by desperation into "creating a crisis," the the threefold technique I read about much later in Dr. Howard Clinebell's, "Understanding and Counseling the Alcoholic through Religion and Psychology," Jack would have died years earlier of alcoholism. The shock of having his whole world collapse about him simultaneously—job, family and health—finally forced him to face reality.

For the first year of sobriety, our family tiptoed around the house and catered to Jack's every whim. I never before realized my gift for play-acting—dubious as I was that this miracle could last, I never displayed a moment's doubt or fear. Gradually the pretense became a reality and I knew that AA therapy would keep my husband sober so long as he would accept the offered help.

Years of gradual withdrawal from any close circle of friends had taken their toll. Jack's sobriety alone was not enough to change me from a worried, fearful and deeply insecure individual, whose reactions during his active alcoholism may have had a more drastic effect on our son and daughter than *his actions*. I was so lacking in confidence that it took all my courage to pick up the phone one day and call an absolute stranger to ask for help. This was the mother of a school chum of my son's, whose father was also an AA member, The mother belonged to something called the "family group."

It was there I learned I was expecting too much too soon, that for the wife and husband facing a sober marriage after many years of alcoholism, the nonalcoholic partner's expectations for happiness are often unrealistic and idealistic. It would take time and real effort on my part to recognize and gradually repair the damage to my own personality, and those of our children. The Al-Anon program helped our marriage become what I had always dreamed it would—a maturing of two people into a happy give and take and the restoration of mutual respect. I was no longer fearful of enjoying life. There were numerous other rewards, the paramount one being a return to faith in a Higher Power, who shows us the way when we are in greatest need.

## But for the Grace of Al-Anon

I have lived now for twenty-three years with an alcoholic. Had I known anything at all about alcoholism that long time ago, things might have been different. My mother was concerned about Jim's drinking when we were engaged but I assured her she needn't worry—he could stop any time. I was sure he could because he said so.

When it continued, and worsened, after we were married, I went through all the phases: blaming myself for it, trying to prevent it, trying to hide it and making myself generally into a person totally unlike my former self.

Finally, about eight years ago, I was desperately unhappy and no longer willing to live such a dreary life. From somewhere I remembered hearing about AA and spoke that familiar piece about "It's AA or else." So, for a time it was AA. For almost a year, after initial difficulty, AA *was* the answer and we attended meetings regularly. For the first time I found a place where I could speak freely to other wives.

The things I heard in meetings were totally new to me. If I had read things in newspapers about jails, crimes and misbehavior, I had never related them to drinking. I had not realized that overindulgence in alcohol was an illness. It was a comfort to learn that Jim was not entirely responsible for his conduct.

But before the year was over, so was my new-found peace. And all that I had heard in other men's stories came back to haunt me ten-fold. A wet brain was something new to worry about; so was the worry over Jim's assaulting someone when he was not responsible and didn't even know what he was doing. The idea of preventing his taking the first drink became my first thought. I was the complete eager beaver in selling the program to him.

I know that life with a alcoholic is most difficult for those who have children. I tried my best to protect our child from the effects of her father's excessive drinking. For I did want her to have a normal home, a decent place for friends to visit, and a father she could respect.

For the next five years I moved heaven and earth to help my husband find sobriety. It is needless to say here that nothing that I did helped and most of it harmed. When I heard the Al-Anon Family Groups' Clearing House needed volunteers, I went, not to help myself, but because I had been told the two or three who were working there were struggling to do a job which would swamp a dozen. For the first time some real appreciation of my situation began to dawn on me.

Because the AA program had been presented to me as a way of life for alcoholics, I had not thought to live it myself. I had merely recognized it as a wonderful philosophy for alcoholics, a blueprint for a way to sobriety. But at the Clearing House I learned that Family Groups all over the world were living it themselves, non-alcoholics getting mentally sober through the Steps. I joined a Family Group and learned more of the program as it applied to me.

For me the First Step was the most difficult. I admitted I was powerless over alcohol but I did not accept all its implications. In my own mind was always the nagging thought that there was something I hadn't tried that would work magic for us. Consequently I gained only part of the benefit.

After several years in the Family Group, I really took that First Step. I cannot say what enabled me to do so—perhaps it just took that long for me to learn exactly how powerless I am. Perhaps I had to suffer the extra time in order to appreciate what havoc I was adding to an already difficult situation. But with the taking of that Step, the rest fell into place. I've often watched our cat and thought how much like him I was. He continually catches sight of his tail, bites it, then lets go quickly when it hurts. The only difference between me and the cat is that I held on so long, hurting myself so constantly.

When I took the First Step, I really looked to God for help for the first time. Before that I had been occupied with telling Him what to do, how to do it, and please to do it quickly. I'd always said "Thy Will be done" but hadn't thought I was still striving for my own will. My will, since I was asking only for peace, decency and a normal home, seemed all right to me.

Now I am willing to believe I didn't earn congratulations for the way I had lived my life, and that God could do a better job of running it. I saw that if I hadn't fought against alcoholism, that problem might have been solved earlier.

I had made Jim obstinate by pushing too hard. If I had just given up earlier in my efforts to control his drinking, our home would have been more tranquil, at least by the measure of my own acceptance and serenity.

We are still living with the problem. Perhaps Jim is one of the unfortunate few who will never get the program. That is not for me to say, just as I cannot say how long I can continue life under present conditions. But I am now able to live with more grace, more acceptance and more happiness. The times between bouts are not clouded with worry about the next episode. I have learned to live through his binges by detaching myself from them. I have learned not to scold, make scenes, become depressed or to chase after Jim. I have stopped pouring out liquor, have stopped sleeping on the floor in front of the door so he can't get out for more. I have stopped all the useless schemes I used to try.

I have learned to trust that God in His own time will help us both, as He sees fit and that no matter what happens it is possible to be a better person for having lived through these difficult years. There are a lot of things I'd be glad to have changed in my life— I'd like to be free of debt, I'd like to have a little financial security and I'd like to have a husband who is always himself. But I have learned that just living is not the most important thing. I am concentrating on *how* to live my life as it is, and not necessarily as I'd like it to be.

With the help of God and the AA and Al-Anon Steps, I am constantly trying to live His way—and not mine.

The foregoing was written five years ago and little has changed except that the opening sentence should read, "I have now lived with an alcoholic for more than thirty years." It is possible to say this only because of Al-Anon. Without its teachings I would long since have given up the struggle and cried quits. But once having accepted the idea that alcoholism is a disease, I have never felt free to leave since I know in my heart that if Jim suffered from any other ailment, no matter how personally demanding, I'd have seen him through it without question. I cannot see that alcoholism is any excuse for me to leave him. I have no quarrel with others who feel differently but as in all Al-Anon, this is my own decision to make.

I hope and pray that some time Jim will really return to AA and live it honestly and wholeheartedly. I hope that day comes soon. But it is because of Al-Anon and those early days at Headquarters, that I have such hope.

### Al-Anon Is My Leveler

"Why do you need Al-Anon? After all, your husband has been sober for ten years. Isn't that enough for you?"

Time and again since I came into Al-Anon two yeas ago, I have been asked these questions by wives of long-standing members of AA. I've had plenty of time to find the answers I couldn't always make in person to women who seemed so sure they needed nothing but AA.

When I first joined an Al-Anon group, I was in a state of utter chaos. My biggest resentment was AA. My husband's road to sobriety was straight and true because he was working at it a day at a time. My road to emotional sobriety was at a dead end because I never really thought to apply the Twelve Steps to myself. Many, many times I took his inventory. I felt I had lost my individuality and identity. At AA meetings, during coffee time, on meeting people, I would be introduced as N's wife, never by my given name. I did so resent it; I felt so left out. Imagine resenting the only thing I'd ever wanted, my husband's sobriety. That truly is insanity.

All this has changed since coming into Al-Anon because my attitude has changed. I now have that wonderful feeling of belonging, of being accepted. I wish I could reach other wives of the "old timers" who think they don't need Al-Anon, because I know the state some of them must be in.

This second chance I've been given to clear the wreckage of the past is beyond comprehension. But I will work at it a day at a time, because now I understand me, and by applying this suggested program to myself a day at a time, I can keep small hills from becoming mountains.

The Al-Anon program is my leveler.

### Alcohol Is Not My Problem

I have made a startling discovery: Alcohol is not my problem. Alcohol can only be the problem of an alcoholic. However, through living with an alcoholic over a period of years, I became as sick mentally, physically and spiritually as he.

My husband's illness has a definite name and treatment. *He* is an alcoholic, and Alcoholics Anonymous is his program of recovery. *My* maladjustment was a little more difficult to name and treat, but I was definitely neurotic.

I am grateful for all the experiences I have had. I am deeply grateful for the privilege of associating with others in Al-Anon who have had similar experiences, because I have learned that the love and friendship which is the basis of our lives, and our way of life, needs the *best* we have, *all* the time.

I do know that for every alcoholic there is a wife or husband, often children and a mother and father, whose lives have become as troubled as that of the alcoholic himself. If I can help one man or woman to deal realistically with his or her alcoholic mate, then I may have helped that alcoholic and at the same time given hope and encouragement to his loved ones.

Knowing nothing about Alcoholics Anonymous and much less about alcoholism, my mental processes deteriorated as rapidly as those of my husband. Gradually we lost all the fine things we had hoped and planned for and had within our grasp. This developed in me a confusion which continued to engulf me with each succeeding failure in my attempts to help him.

Throughout all these bad times there did remain within me a faith that sometime, somehow, something would help my husband find himself and be the fine person I knew and loved in his sober times. There is a dominant force in the lives of some of us that refuses to let us abandon our mates, even in the darkest hours.

Ill in mind and body, I found myself in a hospital, recovering from major surgery. Despite well-meant promises not to drink at that time, my husband drank himself into another hospital on a ten-day bender. This was the physical and mental low for us. While in the hospital I was informed that my husband had been in touch with Alcoholics Anonymous at his own request, and that he believed he had found a way out. My immediate reaction was one of "tongue-in-cheek" disbelief. By this time I hardly cared what happened.

Coincident with my convalescence, my husband soberly and eagerly attended AA meetings. For the first time I heard him say, "I can never drink again. I am an alcoholic." Believe me, I was still a long way from being convinced that anyone or anything could ever help him. I had had a thousand promises in a thousand different ways. I was afraid to believe. I don't think I shall ever forget the day, shortly after I came home from the hospital, when two Al-Anons, wives of AA's, came to see me, two happy women who said, "Six months from now you'll be laughing at this." Fortunately, I had neither brickbats nor the strength to wield them that day.

With the advent of AA in our lives, that faith gave rise to hope and when we dared hope, our confusion and despair began to vanish. We could begin to think with clear minds.

With my recovery and first attendance at an AA meeting, I began casting about for information about alcoholism. At Al-

Anon meetings I learned through listening to the experiences of other non-alcoholic mates that, by utilizing the Fourth of the Twelve Steps, I could discover many distinct neurotic tendencies in myself, acquired in my days and years of dark confusion.

The Fourth Step, which reads, "Made a searching and fearless moral inventory of ourselves," is a real challenge to honesty with one's self. We all find it so easy and pleasant to view ourselves through a rosy hue of complimentary half-truths, and we find it so hard and unpleasant to take a look in the uncompromising and glaring light of the unvarnished truth. If I were to help my husband in his efforts to recover, I could do so only by effecting my own recovery. I saw my husband daily striving to live a program of deep spiritual regeneration and I knew I must do likewise.

Here came the fruition of that deep faith that had sustained me. My sincere desire to help would no longer be doomed to disappointment. I needed only to improve myself. From that day to this the principles and philosophy of the AA program have been the governing influence in our lives. I removed my tongue from my cheek and put my nose into the AA book and Al-Anon literature. I was convinced that something wonderful was happening in my life. It was then I saw, I heard, I believed. Thus came hope.

We must realize that the recovery of our own mental and emotional health does not occur overnight, no more than the recovery of our alcoholic mates. Even as they, we can grow by learning and applying to our own lives the principles of the AA way of life. How many times in our despair we have said, "I would do anything if my husband would only stop drinking"? Now is our opportunity to prove our sincerity by continuous action to do the only thing in which we can reasonably hope to succeed: improve ourselves, our home lives, and our spiritual attitudes.

We gradually understand we must relinquish the martyr role for a more realistic one in the light of our philosophy of living. Many adjustments must be made in our transition from a person "wronged" to that of a person who may have *been* wrong. It is our obligation to learn the difference, and there is only one way to do that: "Know thyself!"

Honest, sincere study and application of the AA and the Al-Anon program, coupled with the friendship and fellowship of those who have shared our experiences, provides regeneration of body, mind and spirit. It is the spirit of the AA philosophy that catches and holds the alcoholic and non-alcoholic alike.

It is because of this spirit, this influence, that the alcoholic grasps that life-line in his search for release from physical pain and the attainment of peace of mind and serenity of heart and soul. The non-alcoholic has shared in this search. I believe that a person who attains peace of mind is well on the way to recovery from any maladjustment. He who possesses peace of mind must have an honest faith in a Power greater than himself, faith in himself and in those about him.

"To thine own self be true, and it must follow, as the night the day, thou canst not then be false to any man." We must be absolutely courageous in our honesty with ourselves. We are attempting to keep stride with an individual who must practice rigid honesty in all things. Deceit has no place in his new life and is therefore more easily recognized in the actions of others.

There is a humorous story of a conversation between a pastor and a member of AA. The pastor inquired, "Don't you have hypocrites in AA?" To which the AA member replied, "Yes, but we have it on you. We can *smell* ours."

Constant or recurring self-pity for wrongs or fancied wrongs that may have happened in the past is destructive. You might just as well close the door on yesterday because it is gone. It is too late to go through that day again. We are happiest when, in spite of discouragement, we put up a good home front. It is an exacting task, not made up of occasional glamorous gestures, but of a steady self-discipline, sensitive awareness of what hurts, what irritates, what displeases.

When our self-pity takes the form of criticizing the former character defects of our alcoholic mates (before AA) which he is now striving to overcome, it might be well to take the recommendation of the Sioux Indians, "Oh, Great Spirit, help me never to judge another until I have walked a mile in his moccasins." A friend of mine also showed me that each time I used a finger to point out a fault in someone else, three fingers point back at me.

Each of us will have come a long way when we can approach every activity in our lives with the AA prayer ever in mind: "God grant me (not only my husband) the serenity to accept the things I cannot change, courage to change the things I can (mostly me), and wisdom to know the difference." Just for twenty-four hours!

### The Beginning of Understanding

I am the wife of an alcoholic. When I first came to Al-Anon I was defeated, fearful, lonely and frustrated. Resentment filled my thinking, warped my judgment and paralyzed my usefulness. Because my own problem filled my mind so completely, I found myself forgetting appointments, going blocks past my bus stop, looking at people and not hearing what they said.

When no one in the group said anything about how to deal with my alcoholic husband, I was surprised and disappointed. I was shocked and even more resentful at the suggestion that perhaps I might need some reconditioning of my own thinking and way of living.

That phase passed. As I learned more, I began to appreciate that I actually was powerless over alcohol, even as my husband seemed to be, and that it made sense to turn this problem over to a Power greater than myself. That was the beginning of my understanding of the importance of the first two suggested Steps in the AA program which apply so perfectly to non-alcoholics like ourselves. This understanding brought peace of mind and a new joy of living I would not have believed possible. Yet nothing had changed but my own attitude.

I used to wonder why *my* prayers were never answered. Now I can see that they were completely selfish, that I was not ready, spiritually, for them to be answered. How could I expect to have answers to my prayers when I was filled with hostility, self-pity and resentment?

I became aware of my own defects and what I could do to change them. I "let go and let God." I substituted positive thoughts for negative ones—love for enmity, praise for criticism, forgiveness for resentment. Working the Al-Anon program on a twenty-four hour basis, with daily time for prayer and meditation, gave me new confidence and faith. And I have found, as I was told I would, that "right answers" do come when you put your mind on "being" rather than on "getting."

### Helpful Reality

When I say that I am the most grateful woman alive and that the alcoholic problem is still unsolved in our home, you may think I don't know what gratitude means. But I am truly grateful for what a "Power greater than myself," working through Al-Anon, has done for me.

I once lived in a state of despair and defeat. My fear for my husband, for what alcohol was doing to him, amounted to panic.

Not understanding that his drinking was a symptom of illness, I was filled with resentment and self-pity. I was literally a sick person myself.

Then I heard of AA but could not interest my husband in it. One day I asked an AA member if the program had helped him. His brief answer startled me. "God has helped me," he said. I was unprepared for such an answer. Previously when some one had brought God into a conversation, I had been uneasy and embarrassed. But when this man spoke of God as a helpful reality, it did more for me than all the sermons I had ever heard.

I began to believe that if God could help this man, He could help me. As soon as possible I sought out an Al-Anon group. I shall always be grateful for the heartwarming friendliness of those women who had been through the same experience as mine. There was no need to detail my troubles to them, or to try to hide them. Everyone understood. It meant that I could relax and be natural. The small spark of courage and hope kindled by my first AA friend was fanned into flame.

My greatest help came when my new friend told me, "Take your hands off your husband's life entirely. Turn that problem over to God as you understand Him. Then begin to do something about your own life."

I was told that my life would change in proportion to the honest effort I made to change it. I said to myself, "If that is the secret of the serenity I see in the faces of these people, that is what I want." I had reached the end of my rope; I was absolutely defeated and discouraged. I was ready to do anything these kind people suggested.

I found that trying *not* to run my husband's life was easier said than done. Dreading disaster, fearful for his safety, I had been trying for years to save him from himself. Today I realize that this attitude had probably only made things worse. And when I wanted with all my heart to "let go and let God," I found myself bound by years of wrong habits.

The change in me and in my attitude came very gradually. I often had to learn to control my tongue when angry. I had to learn not to question erratic comings and goings. I had to ignore evidence of drinking. I had to put aside doubts that everything would turn out for the best. Over and over, I had to remind myself, "He is in the hands of a Power greater than I am; things will work out."

Gradually I discovered that concern over the alcoholic problem no longer occupied my mind to the complete exclusion of other things. I began to experience a feeling of release. I knew that I was free of a burden and responsibility that were too heavy for me. I sensed that our lives were being guided by a Power that was infinite and loving. I felt a lightening and buoyancy of spirit that brought with it a strong sense of security. Finally I realized, "Why, I really am as free as the air." It was a tremendous feeling.

Formerly, every reminder of my husband's drinking set off a terrific surge of bitterness and resentment. I learned that I had to overcome this weakness. I did, but I can't claim all the credit. Today, when I ask for help from the Higher Power we speak of in Al-Anon, I can feel a change within myself. The hateful emotions are replaced by patience and loving kindness. I find it easier to live with myself since I have replaced negative thoughts with positive ones. It should not be difficult to understand the gratitude I feel. For I am grateful for the opportunity to learn and live this new way of life.

STORIES OF HUSBANDS

*Al-Anon the Clinic*

She lay there with eyelids closed, and the eyelids were a most unnatural red. Her face was white and still; on it was the shadow of death. She smelled of alcohol. The whole room smelled. But she slept, and I was grateful for that.

I am her husband, the person incarcerated with her in this prison, this tomb of alcohol and despair. I have often wondered about the indecency of my relief at moments like these. It was all right for me to be glad she had not killed herself, that she had another chance. But I also was glad, at whatever price, whatever the drug the doctor had given her, for these few hours of relief from the antics and agony and self-destruction of an alcoholic.

An alcoholic. It seemed impossible that my wife should be an alcoholic. She is a very fine person when she is not crazed by alcohol. She is poetic and artistic; she has more actual knowledge and sensitivity than any person I have ever known. She is a descendant of a signer of the Declaration of Independence; she is related to a whole flock of illustrious pople.

"Don't you ever think of that?" I once asked, "when you start to drag the whole thing in the mire?"

"Oh yes, I think of it," she replied. There were moments when she was as much in danger of dying of remorse as of alcohol. "I'll kill myself," she said, and more than once she had tried.

In fact, that was why she drank, at least part of it, to get the oblivion of alcohol. Sometimes, in the midst of drinks or in the midst of our arguments, she wanted to jump out of the window.

"It seems to me," she once said after a drunk, "that I've ruined everything—your love, my own immortal soul."

"Then why do you drink?"

She shrugged. Even if you got to the bottom of it, what difference did it make?

Now she slept and I thought, "How much more can I take?"

I owed her something, and not only the marriage vow. Her great mind and her great spiritual resources had helped me with something no one else had helped. Like her, I have a suicidal impulse and, like her, I have had it since childhood. It was one thing that had brought us together: we understood each other. She had taught me how I could get hold of the first twist of the suicidal impulse before the whole thing knotted and knotted and almost drove me mad. I was grateful that she had cured me. That was what I owed her.

"But I've paid off," I said to myself.

"When do you pay off?" the inner voice asked. The only answer was the smell of the room and the stirring of the drunken hand reaching for sleeping pills. Sometimes in her alcoholic agony she would take a whole handful of sleeping tablets. She had them hidden around the house as she hid alcohol. Sometimes, getting up to look for alcohol, perfume, or rubbing alcohol, she would ask, "Do you think I'll go blind?" Drugged by drink, by hypodermics, or by sleeping pills, she would fall, crashing her head on the tile floor of the bathroom.

Once, when we lived in the country, drunkenly searching the barn for whiskey when I was away, she had fallen on a board full of rusty nails. When she was taken to a doctor, his wife, a former nurse, fainted at the sight.

And now I thought: "I've done it. It doesn't matter if I love her. It doesn't matter what she's done for me. I admit all her virtues. All the same, I can't take it."

In the morning I started to pack.

"Where are you going?" "Away."

"Don't leave me." She struggled piteously for her senses. "Don't leave me. I'm so alone."

It did not mean that she had no friends. I knew what she meant; it was our deep understanding and a relationship you cannot have with many people.

But that did not keep me. "I can't take it any more," I said.

"I don't blame you. I'll kill myself."

"It's beyond your threats," I said. Then I thought of something. There was a woman who lived not far away, a woman my wife had long befriended. I called her and told her I was leaving.

"Why don't you call AA?" she said.

"You know we've tried that," I said. "It didn't work."

"It's only one call," our friend replied. "What's one minute after all these years?"

So I tried, saying to the person who answered the phone at AA, "Please send someone with a sensitive nature, someone with a spiritual quality. My wife won't respond to any other kind."

So Emmie came to our house, a great lady who had herself nearly sunk in the sea of alcohol, and who had survived to help others.

After six months of sobriety on my wife's part, Emmie confessed, "When AA told me you wanted someone intellectual and artistic, I wore my Phi Beta Kappa key and you never noticed it."

"No," my wife answered smilingly, "but we did notice your golden personality."

Emmie was responsible for my getting into Al-Anon. I had found out that I had no power over alcohol, but I had never heard the statement put so clearly. However, in Al-Anon I found something more persuasive than ideas. I found people who had lived through some of what I had experienced, people who eased some of my worst feelings.

For one thing, I was suffering remorse for my actions. Once I had struck my wife. I do not believe in that sort of thing; it is a violation of my principles. It is also a part of the contagious insanity of alcoholism. When I confessed at a meeting that I had struck this woman so dear to me, another member said, "That's nothing. Once I was so mad at my husband when he was drunk that I pushed my cigarette into him. When he woke up he asked innocently, 'I wonder how I got that burn?'"

That may not be funny, but we laughed, and already at that first meeting there was established an element of sympathy and understanding in the fellowship. But Al-Anon is much more than that. At the second meeting, when I was asked about my feelings towards my wife who was then in the hospital, I said: "I'm thinking of leaving her."

"Have you considered the Fourth Step?" someone asked.

"What is it?" I had read it and forgotten what it said.

"Take another look at it," my friend insisted.

It is the Step suggesting a fearless moral inventory of oneself. This was not complete news to me. I had done it, but not often. Not recently.

It is, I suppose, the most difficult of all the Steps. And it is perhaps the most rewarding. When one is married to an alcoholic, there is the inclination to put all troubles at the alcoholic's door. But the truth is that (along with our capacity to love and to honor) we bring to these relationships all the flaws with which we were born into this world, and those we have picked up on the way. My conduct toward the alcoholic had been far from perfect. My conduct toward my fellow man and toward myself had been far from perfect.

More than anything else, Al-Anon to me is a clinic where we

can reconstitute our own emotions and relationships. It is not always like that, of course. I have seen Al-Anon meetings that were more like a ladies' sewing circle. There is a great freedom in Al-Anon.

Al-Anon gives its members more freedom than any group I know. You do not have to say the Lord's Prayer if you don't want to If you do not wish to contribute or are not able to when the basket is passed, no one will care. Even the Twelve Steps are only "suggested."

I know of no other organization where the fundamental subject is life. Living with an alcoholic puts you up against the essentials of life, whether to pay the rent, whether to stay married any longer, what is to be considered in someone else's soul, what is to be considered in your own. In these terms I think of Al-Anon as a clinic, one where I have seen people come to sanity, among them myself.

I must also report that after nine months of sobriety, my wife has had a slip. It causes me, in this moment of writing, an amount of pain. But I can also say that in these nine months our life has been reborn, hers in AA, mine in Al-Anon. In spite of this slip she can, and I believe she will, go on to long-lasting sobriety in AA. Out of pain we made great joy. And I expect that we shall have it again.

### Thanks to Al-Anon

We who have been helped and been given so much through the programs of Alcoholics Anonymous and the Al-Anon Groups have reason to be extremely grateful. First and foremost I am thankful to God and grateful to AA for my wife's sobriety, and secondly I am grateful that I, as a non-alcoholic husband, can share this new-found way of life with her.

Drinking presented no problem during the first ten years of our married life. During this time we both took a few drinks on occasion and could have been classed as social drinkers. I did not realize what was happening when my wife began to drink alcoholically. There came the time, however, when I knew that she could no longer control her drinking. She could not stay sober for any given time, or at any specific time.

As I look back on our life then, I thank God for giving me the faith and the strength to believe that somehow, somewhere, we could find a solution to this problem. There were many occasions during this drinking period when it would have been much easier to walk out, destroy our marriage and leave her to find her own solution. Again, I say, "Thank God," for guiding me away from such courses.

As the drinking got worse, I tried every way possible to evolve the perfect situation to induce sobriety. At my suggestion we tried what we now know to have been a geographic cure. We moved back to our home state, near the family and old friends, where we might also meet and associate with new friends. But in a short time we were withdrawing and repelling all offers of friendship.

I tried threats of hospitals and commitment, coupled with bribes of material things, if only she would stay sober. At my insistence we tried doctors and psychiatrists. There was a short confinement in a hospital, after which the drinking got worse. We were not told that we were dealing with illness, and most certainly it had not occurred to me. I was sure that she could stay sober if only she would use her will power.

At the suggestion of an attorney, my wife made her first contact with Alcoholics Anonymous. She had definitely decided that I was the contributing factor to her excessive drinking, and she felt that divorce would be the solution. (We can laugh about that incident now; in most cases the non-alcoholic files for the divorce.) As a result of her association with AA, however, the divorce proceedings were stopped.

The first attempt at the AA program was not successful, but it was a beginning. We have both since learned that the alcoholic must have a desire to stop drinking and be willing to do something to help himself. Nevertheless this initial exposure did give me the first real hope that there was help for our dilemma. Here were people who understood. I was no longer completely alone in my frustration and despair.

Our local Al-Anon Group was just being formed, and I attended a few meetings, but always with the idea in my mind that everything would be fine if only my wife would change her ways. Little did I realize that I, too, could benefit by applying the principles of this new way of life to myself.

For several months she continued her research into drinking and I did absolutely nothing about trying to change myself. Then came the time when she became willing to accept the fact that she could no longer drink as she would like and made her own decision about attending the AA meetings and applying the Twelve Suggested Steps to her life.

The first month of her continuous sobriety was probably the most trying time of all for me. I was ever fearful that something I might say or do would upset her. Suddenly it dawned on me that I was powerless where alcohol was concerned, and certainly I had permitted my life to become unmanageable. I had completely missed the point that alcoholism is an illness, and with the bloated ego that we husbands sometimes have I had dwelt on the hope that I could find the answer to her problem. Fortunately, I soon learned that she could find her own solution in the program and fellowship of AA, and that my help could come through the fellowship of Al-Anon.

So I began attending Al-Anon meetings (in spite of the fact that most of the time I am the only male member present, a situation which I resented in the beginning). I listened to others, and through the group therapy I learned to understand my wife better and what she is attempting to do. I realize that the way I can be most helpful to her is to make it possible for her to keep "first things first." By this I mean, co-operation and a willingness to participate in AA activities with her wherever possible and allowing her to be as active as she needs to be. I keep hoping that more husbands of alcoholic wives will join our Al-Anon groups. There is always the thought that perhaps my mere presence at these meetings may lend encouragement to these husbands to join us.

We are now aware that the slogan "First Things First" is of importance to us as a family. The first thing in our home life is our alcoholic problem, and so long as the alcoholism is arrested, we can live together happily, with a degree of contentment and serenity. I find that the slogans "Easy Does It" and "Live and Let Live" can also have profound meaning. "Easy Does It" reminds me that I should try to live just one day at a time, doing the best I can for each twenty-four hour period, and not to expect too much too soon. There are things I can do, changes I can make so that I may become a better person. These can be accomplished only by "doing it." For a long period of time, I tried to put other lives in order, according to my wishes. I tried to run the show, only to find that my suggestions and ideas were rejected. I can live only my own life, letting those around me do likewise.

The Serenity Prayer clarifies the fact that the only one I can change is myself. This I can do through the application of Steps Four and Ten, and in so doing, along with an honest effort to apply the remaining Steps, I feel I have achieved some measure of spiritual growth. Being willing to try to continue to improve and regularly attending Al-Anon meetings, perhaps I may be able to help others along the way. To me there is nothing finer than to see a new family come into the fellowship we share, and to observe the change that takes place in both the alcoholic and the non-alcoholic. These are God's miracles among us.

Only recently I heard this statement: "I am an alcoholic. I had reached a point in my life where I no longer had the power of choice where my drinking was concerned. Today, thanks to AA I have that power of choice. I don't have to drink." This came to me over our local radio station, where my wife was one of two members of AA being interviewed, anonymously of course, on a local public service program. "I am an alcoholic." A simple statement, but after more than ten years of continuous sobriety, it never ceases to remind me of the wonder that has been wrought in our lives. The simple statement, "I am an alcoholic," eliminates the past fears, and the frustrations, and the feelings of helplessness and near hopelessness. It reminds me that I need always keep a sense of gratitude for what we have received and what we can share, truly a new way of life. I can only say, "Thanks to God for AA and Al-Anon, and thanks to AA and Al-Anon for showing me God."

## PARENTS SPEAK

### Sobriety and My Son

I am the father of an alcoholic, a boy who now no longer drinks, thanks to AA. Anyone who knew me in the days when Bob was drinking will appreciate that mothers and wives aren't the only ones who suffer in a home where a loved one is a problem drinker.

I have dragged my son out of bars and forced him to come

home with me. Other times, waiting for him to return, I have paced the floor hours on end, hot with anger and resentment.

A doctor told me Bob had an illness, but I thought he was simply excusing the boy. But the doctor also told me about AA; he thought it could help. After making some inquiries, I began going to open meetings—alone. For a long period, Bob refused to go, but I attended regularly. In those days there were no Family Groups, but I soon came to appreciate that the doctor was right; alcoholism was an illness. I stopped chasing after Bob and taking his money and liquor away. I realized that he would have to want to stop drinking before I could help him. I recognized that the first important thing was to change my own attitude and stop fighting my son.

After a while, Bob began to go to AA meetings with me. He must have sensed the change in my approach. Whatever the reason, AA made sense to him right away. He hasn't had a drink since.

When I first heard of Family Groups, I wanted to be a part of the new fellowship. I knew how much they could have helped me had they been in existence during the days when Bob was drinking. I thought, too, that I could help others by passing along my experience in working with an alcoholic close to me. And finally I realized how much I still had to learn about living with a recovered alcoholic.

Nearly twenty years have passed since Bob was restored to his family through AA—twenty years during which we have been richly repaid for whatever trouble we had while Bob was drinking.

Sobriety always brings in its wake a flow of blessings beyond reckoning, and these were very real for us. I look upon them as something in the nature of a loan on which God expects payments to be made in service.

Al-Anon offers the opportunity for such service in trying to carry the message to others, and for this I am sincerely grateful.

### Al-Anon Has Changed My Life

My son is an alcoholic, and my only child. A few years ago everything that made his life worthwhile seemed lost: his wife and children, his job, his health, his relationship to me. Because I have been a widow for many years, George and his wife, and my grandchildren have been the center of my life. Until I found Al-Anon that center seemed like a vortex of despair and unhappiness.

My husband was an army man so George grew up on various posts. He was a bright boy, got high marks in school and particularly in religion. He was graduated from a military academy at fourteen, so young that we kept him on at the academy for another year before he applied for admission to West Point, his keen ambition. He had to drop out because of defective eyesight. That was the first disappointment in his life, a deep one, but he took it without apparent bitterness.

After Pearl Harbor, while my husband was in the south training recruits, George left college and enlisted. He was a captain at twenty-three and came out of the war with a good record. I didn't know then that he had also acquired a record for drinking in the duller periods between active combat.

While he was still in uniform and provided with plenty of money and war anecdotes, he met Sue, the lively, pretty girl who became my daughter-in-law The early years of their marriage before the babies came seemed happy and busy to a bystander, which I tried to be. At parties Sue drank as much as George but without the unfortunate results which began to be apparent within a few years.

There is little use in recounting the details of my son's fairly typical descent into alcoholism. He was a periodic drinker who, when he realized how easily he got drunk, could go for three to six months without a drink. Then some difficulty in his job or daily life upset him, and off he would go on a prolonged bout. The day he met an old academy roommate who was much more successful than he, marked one of recurring episodes that made it clear to Sue and me that George could not take any damage to his pride or the ordinary reverses of fortune.

After lost jobs and several hospitalizations, George called AA for help. I thought that would mean the end of our troubles. I was living with George and his family by this time, trying to help with finances and household tasks. While Sue stayed home in the evenings to be with the babies, I started to go to AA meetings with my son. My faith had always meant much to me so the Twelve Steps made an instant appeal. George was not really ready for AA then, in spite of going to a priest for personal counsel and attending AA meetings occasionally. As soon as he had sobered up enough to be in reasonably good health again, he would start drinking at the first minor disappointment.

Sue and I did everything that we thought would help George. I know now that most of the things I did were wrong. I nagged him, reproached him for neglecting Sue and being such a poor father to three small children, poured his liquor down the sink, and in general treated him as if he were a teenager.

Then someone in AA urged me to go to Al-Anon. At first I went reluctantly. I have never discussed my personal problems; on an army post, you learn that everyone knows too much about your affairs at best. I found I couldn't talk much at meetings, but

I did start to listen. I heard of other women, mothers as well as wives, who had lived through the same experiences. They seemed able to turn their fears over to God. They seemed able to live a day at a time. And, most amazing to me, they were able to look cheerful and to enjoy all the small things in life.

George did not stop drinking but I stopped treating him like a bad boy. When Sue was on the verge of leaving him for good, I was able to persuade her that he was a sick man, not a brutal or weak one.

It has not been a smooth road to travel but it is climbing upward these days. George began going to AA more regularly after Sue and I stopped adding to his problems. He is still unhappy when he hears of other men who have no better minds or training than he, yet who make more money or hold pleasanter jobs. He has had a serious slip within the last year after a long period of sobriety. But all of us—he, Sue, and I—see hope instead of despair. I no longer live with them, feeling that their personal happiness will be more secure without a mother-in-law, no matter how well-meaning, in their daily lives. Sue has developed into a wonderful mother, and is trying to be an understanding wife. And she and George laugh together as they did in those early years of their marriage.

For myself, Al-Anon has made all the difference in my life. I get something out of every meeting: friendly understanding, fresh ideas, a sense of belonging to a group who try to live by principles that are a constant source of comfort and inspiration to me.

### Three Generations

I'm the wife of an alcoholic and also the daughter of one. For years I worried about the effect of my husband's drinking on our children. One day I asked my boys what they remembered of their father's drinking.

To my surprise, they didn't remember very much. It gave me a shock because my older boy went into the Navy to get away from his father's drinking. He said the only thing he could say was he went into the Navy a boy and came out a man—he came back to a home that was trying to live the AA way and it was so different he forgot all that went before. He did remember all the parties we used to have and how his high school friends used our home as their meeting place. He couldn't remember his father being around at all which really isn't as strange as it sounds: his hours were staggered: one week four to twelve; the next twelve to eight, and then eight to four. Naturally most of the time the children were either in school or in bed when he was around.

My younger son, now eighteen and a recent high school graduate, says the only thing he remembers was that his father used to cry a lot and he always felt sorry for him. I believe it affected him more than he thinks it did, which was probably my fault, not Gene's. I tried constantly to hide the drinking from him and always said, "Now, don't tell your father this" and "Don't tell your Dad that," so when his father asked him a question, he'd lie and it got to be a habit with him. He was about twelve when Gene came into AA. It has taken him until last year to learn how to tell a really straight story, without elaborating.

AA now is a part of our family life and I can see a great change in that boy in the last year. He has been to many AA meetings and understands a lot about it. He still doesn't go to his father first with his troubles; he still seems a little afraid of what he would say because when Gene was drinking, he never had any patience with the boy. Now I always bring his problems out for family discussion, the same way we discuss other family problems.

I am trying to say that I believe living the AA program has conteracted the harm which may have been done to our boys by being brought up in an alcoholic's home. One thing always strikes me funny: On Mother's Day, I always get a card. But on Father's Day, Dad always gets a present! Well, years ago, this might have bothered me but it doesn't any more for which, of course, I'm very thankful.

My older son thinks I made too much fuss about his father's drinking and that some day his dad might be able to take a few drinks. Although we have taken him to AA meetings, he hasn't gotten the program as my younger son has.

Like my children, I believe that being the daughter of an alcoholic didn't affect my early life much, I can remember only a couple of incidents of my father's drinking. Like the night my mother threw a heavy suitcase downstairs as he was coming in the door. It hit the door and Dad at the same time—he went halfway into the living room, in dead silence. I stood paralyzed for a moment and then his voice came roaring out of the darkness: "Who the —— threw that!" I was definitely afraid of my mother after that incident; she didn't even know I'd seen her push the suitcase and it didn't even occur to me that my father was partly wrong, too.

Another was on a trip when we were coming from Europe on an English boat during prohibition; all the bars were wide open; it was the night before we were to arrive in New York; next morning we'd be within the twelve-mile limit with the bars all closed. My father was drinking, of course, and finally came up on deck where Mother and I were and said he was going to jump overboard; he was going to drown himself because we didn't want him any more. I tried to call him back from the rail; then my mother said, "Let him go," and I did. We went below and left him there.

It didn't bother me too much as I must have slept. But next morning I went running up on deck and he was asleep in a deckchair, and I got a feeling of disappointment at finding him there. After a long time it began to bother me again. In fact, it is only since AA that I've thought much about my father because he gave us all up quite a few years ago and we didn't hear from him.

But every time he gets sick—when he thinks he's dying—he gets someone to call me, and I go running, and I'm supposed to get him into the hospital, right away. Just like last winter: we hadn't seen him for seven years when someone called me to say he was dying, so I went. I hadn't even known where he lived though it wasn't far from my home. He was in bed and he looked worse than a bum you might see lying in the street.

I said, "Oh, Dad," and he answered, "Well, I'm so sick." I forgot our program and could have choked him right there because I knew he was just drunk. He was, he said, at the end of his rope. We got him into a hospital and he stayed there four months. It was bitter cold but I went to see him twice a week; he was getting along wonderfully. He began to eat and I was so happy I started to talk AA to him but he didn't want it. He was building up his money—I cashed his Social Security check every month and gave him the money. When he had about two hundred dollars, he wanted to leave the hospital. I asked him if he would go to AA and he said, "No. Bring my clothes. I'm going home." I told him he had no home to go to but he said he'd get a room and he'd be all right. So I took him clothes which I'd had cleaned and pressed for him and next day he left the hospital in a blizzard. That morning when I saw it was snowing and blowing I thought "They'll never let him out today." But they did and we haven't seen him since.

I know now that it's no use. I cannot help him since he doesn't want to help himself, but it affects me more now because I feel sorry for him and for not being able to help him. Through the family group I have learned that each person must make the effort to do something for himself. I say to myself, "I will let God take over." It is a good feeling to be able to say that instead of "Why doesn't He do something about it?" It seems to me when we talk like that, we always get angry because He doesn't; we forget we have to relinquish our own will before we can expect help. I think about my father now, wonder what he is doing, and I feel sorry for him as my own son felt sorry for his father. I know what a wonderful life he could have with us, but he says he is too old to change his life and he will not go to AA.

To get back to our children: we must remember our children are individuals, just the same as we are ourselves. They take to life and its problems in many different ways. Although we can bend them a little, they will go their own way regardless. It is up to us, by living this AA way of life and by continued attendance at Al-Anon meetings, to let them see the happiness to be found in striving to live this spiritual way.

TEENAGE STORIES

### *A Matured Teenager*

I am one of the many teenagers who is the daughter of an alcoholic. My life before Al-Anon was the life of a very confused child. As young as I was, I can still remember that our home was a very unhappy one. I recall bitterness, hatred, and a mother and father who at times were not a mother and father. I can truthfully say that when my father drank I hated him. Even after I witnessed two of his suicide attempts, my feelings were cold and distant.

I was ten years old when my mother attended her first Al-Anon meeting. Noticing the change in her made me want to go to the next meeting. My mother was overjoyed at my response so, arm in arm, we attended Al-Anon together.

That happened four years ago, during which time Al-Anon taught me the acceptance of being an individual and detaching myself emotionally from alcoholism, but *not* from love of parents. Realizing that I am an individual, I can choose to either wallow in self-pity or accept this problem as a matured teenager. My greatest joy recently has been in working with Alateens, trying to encourage them to attend meetings and awaken them to the fact that alcoholism is a disease.

I am a very fortunate girl to have been given the priceless teachings of Al-Anon, teachings which will enable me to face life courageously.

### *I Learned the Twelve Steps Along with My Father*

The main entrance of our home was right next to my bedroom. When Daddy drove up late at night I could, of course, hear him. As he stumbled up the steps and made his way into the house, my little dog Trixie would crawl under the covers and go down to the foot of the bed and shake. I'd cover my own head and pray that he'd make it up to bed.

I don't remember when this started but I remember when it stopped. That was after my dad's first AA meeting. I went with him to his second meeting. So did mother. There were no other girls of my age at the meeting.

I was twelve years old. From that time on I attended almost every meeting of the Gulf Coast group until I was seventeen years old. The point I'd like to make is: start out as a family behind the alcoholic in your home. Since you are trying to accomplish a big thing together, you need unity.

Every child wants to believe in his or her parents. When one of them is sick with the disease of alcoholism the child should be given the privilege of finding out that it *is* a disease, not just weakness of will power. Even a small child can understand the meaning and the beauty of this program.

I learned the Twelve Steps and the Serenity Prayer along with my dad. I was helped by hearing the stories of other men and women who told of the same things happening to them that had happened to my own father. They showed me that he was not the only one who had this problem, and they also gave me the hope that in AA he could become the person he wanted to be, with Mother and me to understand and give him our support and trust. The Serenity Prayer has meant more to me through the years than any other one thing.

As a child I didn't want to go to church or Sunday school because people sometimes spoke to me about my father, and this made me ashamed. Thus I lost out on the great building part of my life, the religious part. It was through AA that I got my foundation in spiritual matters.

When a Family Group was formed in our area, I was much interested. I was impressed by the love of these wives and husbands for their partners who needed help. The non-alcoholic also needs help, and Al-Anon is a great outlet for their troubled emotions.

If there is anyone interested enough to give a guiding hand, it isn't difficult to start an Alateen group. I helped start two groups. At meetings we talked of our own experiences, of our fears and of our love and desire for ill parents to be well again. Our programs were based on those of AA and Al-Anon. We used the Twelve

Steps, the prayer, and any other literature we could get, and the monthly *Grapevine* and The *FORUM*.

I sincerely believe that young people should attend as many regular AA and Al-Anon Family Group meetings as possible.

A big help in my case was when I was asked to speak to an AA group. Then when I spoke to a group in New Orleans I was excited to see the prospect of young people also being helped by the program. At first when I went to meetings and state conventions I was the only young person there. Now, however, there are many. It is a big thrill to see great numbers of other people who have lived with this same problem for years and come through so splendidly.

### Excerpts from Alateen Letters

Alateen has helped me at home in many ways. My parents feel that I am a better daughter than I used to be because now I do what they ask instead of first giving them a reason for not doing it.

Alateen has helped me at school in science when we studied about alcohol, and also getting along with fellow students and teachers. It helped me push myself along so as to get into school activities and extra clubs like Youth Fellowship, which is a church activity, also Science Club, and then citizenship clubs put on by the school board and teachers.

Alateen has helped me get to church on Sunday of my own free will, not just because my parents tell me I have to go.

I am the thirteen-year-old son of an alcoholic father. In Alateen I get a true understanding of why my parents or relatives drink. I find this helps me in my school work and outside activities, knowing that it isn't entirely their fault, and that if they are to be cured or even helped, it will take time and understanding.

Before I knew why my father drank I thought of him as a little off because of the way he acted, and I thought that he drank just because he wanted to annoy people. After attending a few meetings of Alateen, I now know the true reason why my father drank.

Before Alateen I used to beef about my father's drinking, stamp out of the house and make a big fuss about it. Now I understand that my father is sick and that it will take a long time for him to get well. Also, Alateen has helped me to get along with the other girls in school and in my social life. I have learned to take my father's moods a lot better. I enjoy coming to Alateen very much.

I am a twelve-year-old girl. Before I started to come to Alateen I felt very sorry for myself. I thought my parent was always wrong and I was the only one who had this problem. Now I feel completely different. I know that I had the wrong attitude myself and that there are many others who have a father who drinks.

The preceding stories are but a few of the hundreds which, each year, are told at Al-Anon meetings or sent in to the World Service Office. There are as many different situations as there are human beings to experience them, but the emotional impact shows many similarities. At the outset there are fear, frustration, anger, helplessness and despair, which, through the wise and kindly help of Al-Anon, are transformed into courage, confidence and serenity.

CHAPTER XIII

# THE STRUCTURE OF THE
# AL-ANON FELLOWSHIP

Al-Anon is composed of two elements:

1) The program which provides spiritual guidance and inspiration to its members, and

2) The Al-Anon Services which maintain communications and take care of routine operations.

The first is the spiritual core of the fellowship, embodied in The Twelve Steps and The Twelve Traditions.

The Services are structured only to the extent that assures effective functioning and free exchange of information and help. This is explained in detail in *The Twelve Concepts of Service.*

The keystone of Al-Anon is the membership. It is made up of people who are closely associated, by ties of family or friendship, with compulsive drinkers.

The basic unit is the Al-Anon group, which may consist of any two or more individuals who come together for mutual help.

The operation of a group is the responsibility of a set of officers who are elected by the members. Officers are usually changed every three, six, or twelve months, to give everyone an opportunity to serve. The officers are: a Chairman, a Secretary, a Program Chairman, a Treasurer, and a Group Representative. They have no authority over the group. Their functions are described in the next chapter.

Thus far we have a picture of a self-contained unit, operating autonomously. How does the group, this one small cluster of individuals, play its role in the far-flung fellowship of Al-Anon which is made up of more than 24,000 such groups? There are two major lines of communication.

The first, consisting of some 16,000 groups in the United States, Canada and Puerto Rico, are united in the World Service Conference.

The second provision for communication is the World Service Office or Al-Anon Family Group Headquarters which acts as a service center for groups all over the world.

The World Service Conference (WSC) was started on a trial basis in 1961 by agreement of the U.S. and Canadian membership. It proved so successful as a means of sharing experience and solving over-all problems that the Delegates decided, in 1963, to make the Conference a permanent feature of Al-Anon.

The Delegates who meet at the annual WSC are elected in such a way that all groups share complete and equitable representation.

Each Al-Anon and Alateen group elects what is known as a Group Representative (GR).

The GR attends District meetings where problems are discussed and information is exchanged. A District is one segment of an Assembly Area in a state or province. It is usually at the District meeting that the GRs elect a District Representative to represent the District.

DRs and GRs are expected to attend all meetings of the Area Assembly when they are called by its Chairman. Once every three years they meet at the Assembly to elect, from among the DRs and its officers, a new set of officers and the one who will serve as Delegate to the WSC for the ensuing three years.

Each World Service Conference Delegate thus represents an

Assembly, each District Representative represents a District, each Group Representative a group.

This succession of links gives each group a voice in the Conference (WSC).

The same links provide a continuous chain of communication between the groups, the WSC and the WSO as streams of information and questions converge on the District meetings and through them to the Assembly and finally to the WSC, so the decisions of the Conference travel back through the same links from Delegate to District Representative to Group Representative and then to the group members.

The WSC takes place annually. The Delegates bring up for consideration all current problems of the Al-Anon fellowship, questions and information which have been placed on the agenda for discussion by the Conference.

The World Service Office operates in conformity with the wishes of the fellowship as expressed by the Conference. It is represented at the sessions by members of the Board of Trustees, and the Executive and Policy Committees.

The World Service Office is the principal service center of the fellowship. All the many functions and activities of the fellowship circulate through it. It is the center, not the head; it serves, but does not control or direct. All of the work at WSO is done by a paid staff, assisted by a number of dedicated volunteers who share the huge volume of work, both creative and clerical. Thousands of inquiries are answered; new groups are given help with their early needs and with the 20,000 groups of the fellowship, as well as with lone members all over the world. In many countries outside the U.S. and Canada, these responsibilities are handled by national service structures. The WSO maintains historical archives; grants permission for and coordinates translation of literature in other

languages; provides assistance for developing national service
structures in other countries; handles public information; pro-
duces and ships Conference-Approved Literature in English and
Spanish. The WSO also publishes a monthly magazine, The
*FORUM;* and the bimonthly newsletters; *INSIDE AL-ANON,*
and its Spanish translation *Dentro de Al-Anon; ALATEEN
TALK; Al-Anon y Alateen en Accion,* a peridoical for Spanish-
speaking members with selections from The *FORUM; AL-ANON
IN INSTITUTIONS,* a triannual newsletter for those in this service; and *LONERS' LETTER BOX,* a sharing vehicle for home-
bound and lone members who do not have a local meeting they can
attend. Other services include looking after the voluminous details
connected with the World Service Conference. In conjunction with
the WSO, many of these and other services are provided for
French-language groups by the Publications Fransaise, P.F.A.
Inc., located in Montreal, Quebec, Canada.

## CHAPTER XIV

# SUGGESTED GROUP STRUCTURE

The setting up of an Al-Anon group is a simple matter; it requires only enough form to assure orderly procedures and division of responsibility.

Each group should have a Chairman and a Secretary. If the group is not large enough to have a Treasurer, the Secretary may act as Treasurer until there are enough members so a Treasurer can be appointed. In a small group the Chairman may also act temporarily as Program Chairman. Officers serve in rotation, ususally elected for a term of six months to a year, but limiting the term of Chairman to one to three months has grown in popularity in many groups.

*Duties of Group Officers*

*The Chairman* opens the meeting with the Welcome or the Preamble, leads the group in the Serenity Prayer, introduces the speakers or announces the subject of the meeting, encourages all the members to take part in discussions, to ask questions or make comments. The Chairman may lead and close the meeting or ask someone else to do so.

*The Program Chairman* suggests topics for discussion and arranges for visiting speakers from other groups.

*The Secretary* is often the link between the World Service Office (WSO) and the group in all routine matters notifying the WSO of changes of address and picking up the mail from the P.O. Box or permanent mailing address. WSO communications and *INSIDE AL-ANON* are sent to the Secretary (or members serving as the groups Permanent Mailing Address) who passes all information along to the members.

The Secretary keeps up to date a list of names, addresses and telephone numbers of all members, orders Conference-Approved Al-Anon Literature and has it displayed at meetings. There should always be enough on hand to distribute to newcomers, to guests, and to professionals who may refer families of alcoholics to Al-Anon.

The Secretary uses the *CONFIDENTIAL* World Directory for mailings to other groups, for Al-Anon purposes ONLY.

*The Treasurer* has the contribution basket passed at meetings, usually during intermission. All contributions are voluntary; members who cannot afford to contribute should never be pressed to do so. All members will want to do their share as their means allow.

The expenses of the group are usually small. They may include rent, literature and refreshments. Whatever surplus remains, after a small reserve for emergencies, is used to support the Twelfth-Step work of Al-Anon. This includes the support of the WSO, the Area Assembly and the local Al-Anon Information Service (Intergroup), if there is one.

The Treasurer keeps a record of all receipts and disbursements and gives a report on the group's financial standing at business meetings. Careful budgeting will keep bookkeeping to a minimum, and will give an idea of the amounts needed for various purposes. The aim should be to have disbursements fairly equal to funds on hand. There is no purpose in accumulating a surplus; it may lead to conflict among the members.

*The Group Representative.* Each group in an Assembly Area should have a Group Representative (GR), to act as liaison between the group and the District and between the group and the Assembly which elects a Delegate to the World Service Conference as described in the preceding chapter. The GR, as the local representative of The *FORUM,* acquaints new members with its usefulness and suggests they subscribe to it and report stories of interest to The *FORUM* Editor.

## *The Advisory (Steering) Committee*

This Committee serves the group by suggesting ideas for public information service and program planning. It may interpret matters of policy and offer solutions for group problems. Membership usually is made up of the group's present officers and immediate past officers. Thus when new officers are elected, membership in the Advisory or Steering Committee changes automatically.

## *The Information Service (Intergroup)*

Where there is a concentration of groups, they may combine to form a local service center, each group electing an Alternate Group Representative who becomes the Information Service Representative (ISR). The ISR attends meetings to unify the member-groups, discuss problems and exchange teams of speakers. Local service centers usually have a telephone listing and a P.O. Box. Volunteers receive calls from people who need help, send them literature and refer them to the nearest group. The center may also handle publicity and institutions work.

# CHAPTER XV

# AL-ANON MEETINGS AND PROCEDURES

The general pattern of Al-Anon meetings is to have a Chairman or leader open and close the meeting and introduce guest speakers, or members who share their experiences with Al-Anon.

Meetings may open with a few moments of silence, followed by the group's reciting the Serenity Prayer. The Chairman or Leader then reads the Preamble or the Welcome to Newcomers or both, reminds those present that the fellowship is anonymous and announces the subject of the meeting. The meeting ends with a suggested closing (see p. 150) followed by a prayer which is said by all who wish to do so.

Meetings usually have a central theme. Even when the session is simply a round-table discussion, more can be accomplished by dealing with a single topic on which each person can express an opinion.

Closed meetings are restricted to members and prospective members—persons who feel their personal lives have been or are being deeply affected by alcoholism in a family member or friend. This gives the participants freedom to discuss their problem and their feelings.

Open meetings may also be held at the group's discretion. They may be attended by anyone interested in the problem of alcoholism and are usually addressed by Al-Anon speakers. Occasionally, speakers are from the clergy or other helping professions. (See page 154.)

Newcomers are especially welcome at Al-Anon meetings; opportunities are provided for the newcomers to unburden themselves and ask questions. When a new member is present the leader usually asks the others to introduce themselves and tell briefly how Al-Anon has influenced their lives. A warm and friendly reception can make the visitor feel a part of the group and encourage continuing to seek help through Al-Anon.

There is no rigid formula for a meeting. Al-Anon speakers identify themselves as relatives or friends of alcoholics. They describe their various attempts to cope with the problem. They tell what they have learned through Al-Anon and how it has helped. Primary emphasis is on the significance of the program and the elements that have been most helpful. Not every speaker's message will appeal to every listener, but there is usually someone with whom the newcomers can identify. Al-Anon Family Groups have helped thousands of men and women achieve a new way of life and many have found help by coming to meetings regularly and keeping an open mind. Opinions and ideas expressed at an Al-Anon meeting are those of the speakers and not necessarily those of the fellowship.

## *Suggested Ideas for Meetings*

1. *Personal Story.* Two or three members are asked before the meeting to tell how they came to believe that the Al-Anon program could help them make a new way of life.

2. *Beginners' Meeting.* Newcomers find help more readily if their introduction to the program is simple and immediately workable. Beginners' meetings give them the fundamentals of the

program and the Twelve Steps and Twelve Traditions with less confusion than if they encounter unfamiliar terms and ideas all at once. Meetings for beginners are usually held 30 to 45 minutes before the regular meeting.

*3. *Twelve Steps*. Some groups review a Step at each meeting. It is more usual, however, to devote an entire meeting to discussion of a single Step, perhaps every third or fourth meeting. The Chairman reads the Step to be discussed. Interpretations can be found in this book and ALATEEN, HOPE FOR CHILDREN, in THE DILEMMA OF THE ALCOHOLIC MARRIAGE or in the booklets: The Twelve Steps and Traditions, or Alcoholism The Family Disease, or The *FORUM*. A guide, called Blueprint For Progress, is available for help in taking a Fourth-Step inventory. Each person present is then invited to make a comment on the Step under discussion and share how it applies to his or her problem.

*4. *The Twelve Traditions*. The group studies one or more of the Traditions and their value in maintaining group unity and growth, keeping in mind the goal of world-wide Al-Anon unity. The procecure for a Twelve Traditions meeting, and the sources of material, are the same as those for the Twelve Steps meeting.

5. *Al-Anon Slogans*. One or more of the slogans may serve as the basis of a roundtable discussion of their value in daily living. References can be found in AL-ANON FACES ALCOHOLISM (the slogans are analyzed in the chapter on "The Working Principles of Al-Anon") or in FORUM FAVORITES.

6. *Panel Discussions*. Two or three members are chosen by the leader or Chairman to sit on a panel and answer questions which have been written anonymously by those present. Their answers often open informal discussion by the entire group; in

---

*Meeting can be based on the discussions found in AL-ANON'S TWELVE STEPS & TWELVE TRADITIONS

this event, the Chairman can help to see that each person has one or two minutes and that no one monopolizes the discussion.

7. *AA Speaker.* An occasional talk by an AA member is interesting and helpful. It should be suggested to the guest speaker that emphasis be placed on adjustments and cooperation at home, rather than to dwell on his experiences as an alcoholic.

8. *Exchange Meeting.* Speakers from another Al-Anon or Alateen group tell their stories.

9. *Family Adjustment Meeting.* Al-Anon, Alateen and AA members discuss the problems of home adjustment after each has joined a program.

10. *Outside Speakers.* Those experienced in the field (clergymen, doctors, social workers, or other professionals) may be asked to speak at an occasional *open* Al-Anon meeting. Too frequent talks by professionals may divert the focus from our own recovery to that of the alcoholic. It is wise to acquaint the speaker with our Traditions.

11. *Literature Meeting.* Al-Anon literature is an inexhaustible source of topics. (See page 155.) Many groups allot one meeting a month to a discussion of a subject from the current *FORUM*, or the book, FORUM FAVORITES, or the many other pamphlets and leaflets which share the Al-Anon/Alateen experience.

12. *Open Meeting.* The function and usefulness of Al-Anon can be explained to a wider audience if an occasional open meeting is planned, to which members, friends, AA members and their friends are welcomed. An open meeting is usually held to celebrate a special occasion or to provide an opportunity for guests to become familiar with the Al-Anon program.

Speakers should be selected with care to make sure they have an interesting and appropriate message. It would be well to make sure that the occasional professional invited to speak at an open meeting is familiar with Al-Anon and its Traditions. Professionals can provide valuable information but it is from Al-Anon members that we hear the ideas and experiences that put us on the road to recovery.

### Planning a Meeting Program

Groups which plan their meetings in advance are more apt to give effective help and encouragement to their members. The Program Chairman, perhaps with the assistance of the Chairman, may plan the topics of meetings in advance. The planned program may then be submitted to the membership for approval and further suggestions. A regular pattern with which the members become familiar is also helpful in encouraging regular attendance at meetings. Some groups give one meeting a month over to thorough discussion of one of the Twelve Steps, another to an article from The *FORUM,* another to a Slogan and a fourth to a Panel Discussion. While such basic patterns may be changed as the members wish, these fundamentals make excellent starting points for sound Al-Anon talk and learning.

The Preamble or the Welcome which follow are read at the beginning of the meeting.

#### SUGGESTED AL-ANON PREAMBLE TO THE TWELVE STEPS

The Al-Anon Family Groups are a fellowship of relatives and friends of alcoholics who share their experience, strength and hope in order to solve their common problems. We believe alcoholism is a family illness and that changed attitudes can aid recovery.

Note: *For Alateen material and meeting procedures see* ALA-TEEN—HOPE FOR CHILDREN OF ALCOHOLICS.

Al-Anon is not allied with any sect, denomination, political entity, organization or institution; does not engage in any controversy, neither endorses nor opposes any cause. There are no dues for membership. Al-Anon is self-supporting through its own voluntary contributions.

Al-Anon has but one purpose: to help families of alcoholics. We do this by practicing the Twelve Steps, by welcoming and giving comfort to families of alcoholics and by giving understanding and encouragement to the alcoholic.

(The Twelve Steps can be found on page 38).

### SUGGESTED AL-ANON/ALATEEN WELCOME

We welcome you to the _____Al-Anon Family Group and hope you will find in this fellowship the help and friendship we have been privileged to enjoy.

We who live, or have lived, with the problem of alcoholism understand as perhaps few others can. We, too, were lonely and frustrated, but in Al-Anon we discover that no situation is really hopeless, and that it is possible for us to find contentment, and even happiness, whether the alcoholic is still drinking or not.

We urge you to try our program. It has helped many of us find solutions that lead to serenity. So much depends on our own attitudes, and as we learn to place our problem in its true perspective, we find it loses its power to dominate our thoughts and our lives.

The family sitauation is bound to improve as we apply the Al-Anon ideas. Without such spiritual help, living with an alcoholic is too much for most of us. Our thinking becomes distorted by trying to force solutions and we become irritable and unreasonable without knowing it.

The Al-Anon program is based on the Twelve Steps (adapted from Alcoholics Anonymous) which we try little by little, one day at a time, to apply to our lives, along with our slogans and the Serenity Prayer. The loving interchange of help among members and daily reading of Al-Anon literature thus makes us ready to receive the priceless gift of serenity.

Al-Anon is an anonymous fellowship. Everything that is said here, in the group meeting and member-to-member, must be held in confidence. Only in this way can we feel free to say what is in our minds and hearts, for this how we help one another in Al-Anon.

## SUGGESTED AL-ANON/ALATEEN CLOSING

In closing, I would like to say that the opinions expressed here were strictly those of the person who gave them. Take what you liked and leave the rest.

The things you heard were spoken in confidence and should be treated as confidential. Keep them within the walls of this room and the confines of your mind.

A few special words to those of you who haven't been with us long: Whatever your problems, there are those among us who have had them too. If you try to keep an open mind, you will find help. You will come to realize that there is no situation too difficult to be bettered and no unhappiness too great to be lessened.

We aren't perfect. The welcome we give you may not show the warmth we have in our hearts for you. After a while, you'll discover that though you may not like all of us, you'll love us in a very special way—the same way we already love you.

Talk to each other, reason things out with someone else, but let there be no gossip or criticism of one another. Instead, let the understanding, love and peace of the program grow in you one day at a time.

Will all who care to, join me in the closing prayer.

CHAPTER XVI

# HOW TO FIND OR START A GROUP

If your peace of mind is lost in anxiety and frustration over the drinking of someone near and important, you can join an Al-Anon or Alateen group. This can be done in one of several ways.

First, you may find a nearby group and attend its meetings. Anyone who feels his or her life has been deeply affected by someone else's drinking is welcome. You can locate a group by looking up an Al-Anon listing in the telephone directory. If there is an Information Service or Intergroup, just call and someone will tell you which group is nearest you and when it meets. Or call any number listed under the name Al-Anon for this information. If none is listed, call AA.

If there is no Al-Anon group in your community, write to Al-Anon Family Group Headquarters, P.O. Box 182, Madison Square Station, New York, N.Y., 10159-0182, for information and literature. Lone members in isolated areas all over the world learn about Al-Anon and how to practice its principles through corresponding with other members. The World Service Office (WSO) can put you in touch with such friends-by-mail.

---

\*In countries other than the U.S. and Canada, registration and other services are often provided by a national general service structure which is linked to the WSO. For local service center addresses write to the WSO.

Or you may start a group along with a few others who need and want Al-Anon help. The procedure is simple.

You decide on a meeting place, which may be in a local church or public meeting hall. You then write to the WSO, announcing the decision to start a group. The WSO will send you the information you need to start with, and a coded registration form which should be filled out at once and returned to the WSO to complete your registration. Once your group is registered, it will receive a starter kit and copies of the bi-monthly newsletter, *INSIDE AL-ANON,* and information about Al-Anon's World Service Conference, in which every group has an important part. You will also be sent a CONFIDENTIAL Directory which lists other Al-Anon/Alateen groups and the name of the World Service Delegate for your Assembly Area.

You and your fellow members should then carefully review all the material you have received, decide who will be Secretary, Chairman, Program Chairman, Treasurer and Group Representative and work out the details of your programs.

It would be well to inform clergymen, doctors, social workers, and others in your neighborhood who have occasion to counsel the families of alcoholics. This can be done either in person or by mail. Be sure to let them know exactly when and where your meetings are held. Some groups announce meetings in a brief, dignified newspaper advertisement; some papers are even willing to include such listings without charge in local events columns.

No dues or fees are required of Al-Anon members, but it is customary to pass a collection basket at each meeting to cover the expenses for the group, for the local Information Service, the Area Assembly, and for the support of the world-wide work of the World Service Office. The group's expenses may include rent, refreshments, and the cost of maintaining a supply of Conference-Approved Al-Anon literature which is ordered from the WSO on a list which comes along with registration information. It is important always to have leaflets and booklets to give to newcomers to enlighten them about Al-Anon. Many groups also order leaflets for local counselors to hand to people who consult them about family alcoholism problems.

As soon as your group can afford it, copies of the nine Al-Anon books can be purchased to be lent to members. These will also provide many ideas on which to base meetings programs. You will find the titles listed in Chapter XVII.

Don't be discouraged if the group grows slowly, or if members drop out. There are many reasons why people do not continue to attend, even if your meetings are highly interesting and helpful.

One way to keep a group fairly intact is to have sponsors for new members. The close relationship between a sponsor and another member helps keep them in touch and encourages the newcomer to attend meetings regularly. The very fact that the sponsor cares enough to call a member and suggest the importance of going to a meeting often overcomes the tug of inertia or personal inconvenience.

The early enthusiasm of some members may dwindle. They may be unable to grasp the idea that they are powerless over alcohol, for example. Or they may decide that they have had all they can get from Al-Anon, not realizing how much it can do for them if they continue. Once the drinking from which they suffered is stopped, they may think Al-Anon has served its purpose; they feel no obligation to help others. Whatever the reasons, Al Anon, like AA, is only for those who really need and want it and these members must be allowed to work out their own problems without pressure or persuasion.

If your group has problems that cannot be resolved by consulting the Service Manuals, you can ask your Group Representative to take the problem to a District meeting or to an Area Assembly. If you need service assistance you can write to the WSO in care of the WSO Staff Coordinators for Alateen, Archives, Institutions, International Coordination, Conference, Literature and/or Public Information.

After the Al-Anon group has become firmly established, serious thought might be given to starting an Alateen group. (See ALATEEN—HOPE FOR CHILDREN OF ALCOHOLICS for details.)

Experienced members may also care to start an Institutions Group to carry the message to families who are in contact with hospitals, courts, mental health clinics, rehabilitation centers, juvenile homes, or penal institutions. Groups meeting at one of these facilities are usually transient in nature and it is essential to have Al-Anon members lead the meeting and, wherever possible, refer families to regular groups near their own homes. (Write to the WSO for help in starting an Institutions Group.)

# Chapter XVII

# AL-ANON LITERATURE

All literature published by the WSO has the approval of the World Service Conference and is so identified. It is suggested that only approved publications be used in studying the Al-Anon program and particularly at Al-Anon meetings.

Al-Anon literature is made available to all Al-Anon groups and to any individual or organization concerned with the problem of alcoholism as it affects the family of the alcoholic:

AL-ANON FAMILY GROUPS
  formerly LIVING WITH AN ALCOHOLIC
AL-ANON FACES ALCOHOLISM
THE DILEMMA OF THE ALCOHOLIC MARRIAGE
ONE DAY AT A TIME IN AL-ANON
FORUM FAVORITES
ALATEEN—HOPE FOR CHILDREN OF ALCOHOLICS
LOIS REMEMBERS
AL-ANON'S TWELVE STEPS & TWELVE TRADITIONS
ALATEEN—A DAY AT A TIME
Pamphlets and booklets on various phases of Al-Anon's influence on the problem. (Catalog available upon request.)
Blueprint For Progress: Fourth-Step Inventory Guide (booklet)
Living With Sobriety: Another Beginning (booklet)
The *FORUM* (monthly magazine); INSIDE AL-ANON;
ALATEEN TALK; AL-ANON IN INSTITUTIONS (newsletters)

# APPENDIX

Talk Given by Bill W. to First Al-Anon World Service Conference 1961

Al-Anon and Its Public Information:
   Newspapers, Magazines and Specialized Publications
   Local TV and Radio
   Al-Anon Speakers at Non-Al-Anon Meetings

# TALK GIVEN BY BILL W.,

CO-FOUNDER OF ALCOHOLICS ANONYMOUS
to the
FIRST WORLD SERVICE CONFERENCE
April 1961

First on behalf of AAs everywhere, I want to bring to this gathering our congratulations and deep affection. There was a time when I could not have done this with equanimity. Many AAs were afraid you were going to crash our exclusive club! But the success of Al-Anon has not only been phenomenal, but I feel it is just about the biggest thing that has happened since AA began.

I know you have approached this new venture with trepidation and misgiving  You have wondered if this Conference will work, if Delegates will really come from the far reaches of Canada and the United States, and how they will work together if they do come. What will the spirit of the Conference be?

These were questions we in AA asked ourselves when *we* held our first General Service Conference in 1951. But our Conference *was* a success and it has continued to have force and effect in all the years since. Sensing the spirit of this meeting, I am sure this will also be the case with you.

In growth, as a movement, you have exceeded anything that ever happened to AA in its early days. And this is, as we all know, because you have been intent on filling the vast vacuum that has so long existed in family relations. We alcoholics, on getting sober, were quickly able to get back to some sort of a job. Now there is a little money in the bank; we are madly active in

157

AA. We make restitution to everybody in the world except the people we have really mauled, and those people are your good selves.

For a long time we all wondered why the "honeymoon" didn't resume. We would say to the wife: "This AA is great stuff; come over to our meetings and get a load of it. We'll even allow you to make the coffee while you warm your hands at the spiritual fires of Alcoholics Anonymous."

Happily, all of that is now in the past; you are commencing to fill, with tremendous rapidity and effect, that awful vacuum that has existed all along, which has affected half of our membership in this close family relation. Of course the family relation is the most difficult one because it's the one that has been the most deformed.

So we AAs, along with our affection and congratulations, do bring you our deep regret, as well as what little restitution we can make at this late date, for the emotional disturbances that our drinking days imposed upon you.

Now comes the time when Al-Anon must function as a whole. You have a dedicated group here. Naturally they had to be self-appointed in the beginning—that was the only way they could get things started. As Doctor Bob and I were known to all AA, so are Lois and her associates here known to you. But this is too thin a linkage for the future. Your services, so vital to the spread of Al-Anon throughout the world, must now be a function of Al-Anon as a whole.

So the deep significance of this small but wonderful meeting, in which history is about to repeat itself, is this:

That you are now applying Tradition Two to Al-Anon as a whole. You Delegates, who have come here as Al-Anon's group conscience, are trusted servants.

True, prodigies of work can be done by mail; prodigies of work can be done through literature. Yet basically it is here, as in AA, that you must finally transact your affairs face-to-face. Now you are face-to-face with your oldtimers, your veterans in Al-Anon's service. You have now become the conscience and guide of Al-Anon, and that is a forward step of the greatest significance, something that should give you deep satisfaction.

Let me emphasize the perils that would surely have beset you had you not begun so to gather. I keep going back to our AA experience. Like yourselves, we AAs had a Trusteeship, a center of service in New York that spread AA throughout the world. People used to say: "Well, this is fine, and it is simple. We'll send in money and you folks will do the work." Therefore when a General Service Conference was proposed for AA, people said: "My God, we drunks can't even run a clubhouse; why should we risk thirty elections of Delegates each year when things are really going along so well?"

But some of us did realize that the oldtimers who operated these AA services could not last forever. We oldtimers are getting to be oldtimers not only in AA years but in natural years. Many of us have only five, ten or fifteen years to go before we cross the Great Divide. We had to recognize that Tradition Two had to have true meaning for the movement as a whole. Hence we recognized that a linkage—a permanent linkage—had to be built between the AA group conscience and its world operations. Thank God you Al-Anons are now seeing that you must do the same. Otherwise a possible future breakdown at your world center could never be repaired. There would be no way to reinstate those vital services unless the Delegate's linkage existed, the kind of linkage you are creating on this historic occasion—the inauguration of your first World Service Conference.

Sometimes you Delegates will come here to give advice; indeed it is in your power to give active direction because the ultimate authority is yours. Then again you will offer suggestions that will make for greater progress. Sometimes you will face momentous questions and problems in which your guidance and collective wisdom will surely manifest itself and save you from grievous error.

At other times you will come here and find internal troubles and you will correct these. At still other times you will have Conference meetings which will be so boring, so dull, that some of you may say: "Why in Heaven's name go to New York just to say 'Yes' to what our public accountant has already verified? This is a lot of nonsense!" But no matter what happens, your presence will insure the maintenance of the all-important linkage. Each one of these yearly meetings, be they dull, be they controversial, is really the insurance policy which can guarantee the future unity and functioning of your society.

May God bless and keep you all. May He set His special favor upon this auspicious beginning. You will surely look back upon this day as a great one in the annals of the Al-Anon Family Groups.

## AL-ANON AND ITS PUBLIC INFORMATION

The fellowship known as Al-Anon has proved abundantly its ability to help those whose lives are troubled by the problem of alcoholism.

Although its tradition rules out *promotion* as a means of spreading its message, it makes use of many channels of communications to *attract* people who need its help: newspapers, magazines, radio, television as well as word-of-mouth.

When we consider the untold millions who need Al-Anon, and who would embrace it if they only knew about it, we realize the importance of using every legitimate and dignified means of getting the word to them.

Because the program is spiritual, and is based on personal interchange of understanding and experience, Al-Anon maintains certain standards in bringing its message to those who need it.

*Newspapers, Magazines and Specialized Publications*

Editors of family pages of newspapers often welcome material about Al-Anon and Alateen which is suitable for feature stories. Personal contacts with these editors has resulted in hundreds of dramatic presentations of Al-Anon's story.

The type of approach that makes a good story is illustrated by the following titles of articles which have appeared in publications in various parts of the United States and Canada.

*"Al-Anons Help Selves, Each Other"*
*"Al-Anon—Hope of the Hopeless"*
*"A Trouble Shared is Cut in Half"*
*"An Oasis Called Al-Anon"*

Excellent and frequent coverage often results from inviting editors to Al-Anon meetings and regional conventions, and providing them with literature.

Feature writers who give advice to troubled inquirers occasionally welcome an opportunity to take up a problem concerned with alcoholism in the family. One such mention, in two articles within a six month period, by a syndicated columnist, brought over 20,000 requests for information to the WSO in New York!

Literally hundreds of *Letters to the Editor* have been accepted for publication; such letters from Al-Anon members are most likely to be used if they relate to a news item of current interest. For example, a story of a family which has come to grief through the compulsive drinking of a parent might inspire such a "Letter to the Editor."

Church publications—magazines, newspapers and bulletins— usually are glad to accept a new angle on a problem of alcoholism in the family.

Magazines frequently discuss alcoholism from one point of view or another. This field is usually open to none but professional writers, but contacts and new ideas can be helpful. Presenting an editor with a really outstanding idea may move him to assign the actual writing of an Al-Anon article to a professional, who can then be briefed and informed by one or more members with sound Al-Anon background.

Many newspapers have current events columns which accept brief notes about an Al-Anon group, its time and place of meeting, with perhaps a short explanatory note about Al-Anon's purposes.

## Local TV and Radio

Appearances of Al-Anon and Alateen members on local TV and radio stations can often be arranged by members, either because they have contacts with station personnel, or because they are creative enough to develop some interesting material for a program.

An Alateen group in California was invited to give an hour-long live program in which the speakers, who were members of Al-Anon, were shown behind a screen so they appeared in silhouette. To protect anonymity still further, they were called A, B and C. Photographs previously taken at an Alateen meeting showed only hands and backs of heads, while the commentator spoke about the program.

## Al-Anon Speakers at Non-Al-Anon Meetings

An important function of local Public Information and Institutions Committees is to arrange or accept engagements for members to speak at non-Al-Anon groups—churches, schools and health care facilities.

There are three points to consider:

1. To speak or not to speak
2. what to say
3. how to say it

Each group will want to decide these questions in its own way, but the following notes may be helpful:

When a request is received to have one or more Al-Anon members speak, it is important to know whether the host organization expects to learn specifically about Al-Anon, or whether more general information about alcoholism is wanted. If the latter, it may be wise to direct the inquiry to AA, a local branch of

the National Council on Alcoholism, a state-sponsored alcoholism center or some other agency concerned with the broader
aspects of the subject.

As in all other phases of Al-Anon public relations, we should
make clear our distinction between *cooperation* and *affiliation*.
According to our Traditions, we are free to cooperate with other
interested organizations in any project or program that imparts
vital information to the public. We never affiliate, however, with
such organizations in joint endorsements or financial involvements. In other words, we may be guests on programs that widen
the understanding of alcoholism as a national health program, but
we do not function as sponsors or fund raisers or engage in any
joint projects. Nor are we free to accept any sort of financial aid,
even when it is offered in sincere good will for such purposes as
defraying printing costs of pamphlets or letters to the public.

Let us now consider Point 1—*to speak or not to speak.*

Al-Anon should welcome the opportunity to carry the message
of hope and fellowship to any reputable groups who seek information *which our experience equips us to give.* Although there is
good reason to be encouraged by the growing public interest in
this subject, there are still vast numbers of people living in desperate alcoholic situations who are unaware of the existence of Al
Anon. Or they may know about it and have only the vaguest idea
of its aims and accomplishments. Well-planned and well-deliv-
ered talks may attract to Al-Anon many who need personal help,
and amplify the knowledge these groups now have of how they
and we may cooperate to advantage.

An Al-Anon member who speaks before an outside audience
should point out that she is expressing her own views and not
necessarily those of the Al-Anon fellowship as a whole. Nev
ertheless, such appearances do enhance the public image of Al-

Anon, which places a considerable responsibility on the speaker and the Public Information Committee. The speaker should try to give a good account of what Al-Anon stands for and how it accomplishes its objectives.

Any Al-Anon member who has been attending meetings long enough to have a grasp of the meaning of the Twelve Steps and Twelve Traditions, who tries to live by them, and who can explain them clearly, is eligible to speak in public. Eloquence is not essential; sincerity and simplicity are. The ability to answer questions and to cope with a general discussion is also important.

Anonymity should be preserved and the identity of the alcoholic protected. The host organization should be reminded that only first names and last initials should be used in advance publicity and in introducing the speaker. In small communities it may be desirable for the group to suggest a speaker from a nearby area rather than a local and therefore recognizable member.

Point 2—*what to say.*

Any Al-Anon member who is preparing to talk before an audience has such a wealth of information on hand that her main problem will be how to select and organize her material.

Find out in advance how much time has been allotted to the speaker and whether this includes a question-and-answer period, often the most meaningful part of the program. The speaker should plan her talk accordingly and run through a timed rehearsal with a member of the Public Information Committee.

Learn as much as possible about the audience. What kind of organization is it? What does it do? Why does it want to know about Al-Anon? How would knowledge of Al-Anon fit into its purpose? Is the group professional, young or old, informed or generally unaware of the problems in an alcoholic home?

Tailor the talk to fit the audience. Stress that Al-Anon does not presume to tell its members, and particularly not outsiders, what to do, but suggests attitudes and actions that have proved helpful.

Should you tell your own story, as you might in a regular Al-Anon meeting? Most non-Al-Anon audiences want to know what Al-Anon is, what it does, how it does it and how they can benefit from this knowledge. Illustrating these points with incidents from your own experience will add color and conviction to your talk, but going into detail about your whole story would probably be too long and inappropriate for a non-Al-Anon meeting.

Make it plain you are speaking simply as an Al-Anon member and not as an authority on alcoholism or mental health. You may be asked some general questions on these subjects which you should be answer intelligently from your reading and study on alcoholism. It might be a good idea to review the chapters on *Understanding Alcoholism the Illness* and *Understanding Ourselves* in this book. In talking to a group of nurses, it may be helpful to review the chapters on *Al-Anon and the Family* and *Al-Anon and the Community.* These chapters are also a good basis for a talk to a group of social workers who frequently come in contact with alcoholism in the home.

If the talk you are going to give is to a group of young people—in high school or college the pamphlets *Operation Alateen, Youth and the Alcoholic Parent,* will be a rich source of appropriate material.

Groups in industry will want to know how they can help the families of their alcoholic employees and what methods have been successful in other organizations. Illustrations from your own experience might fit in well, particularly if at some time or other you were forced into contact with the alcoholic's work situation. If you tell how the alcoholic's drinking affected his work or his associates, it will help your audience recognize the pattern in their own situations.

In speaking to church groups you are well prepared with the spiritual message inherent in Al-Anon's philosophy. This would be an excellent occasion for an analysis of The Twelve Steps as given in this book and in our booklet *The Twelve Steps and Traditions*. Illustrate with incidents from your own experience which show how reliance on your Higher Power worked out difficult problems.

Here is a general outline for a talk which can be adapted to fit the audience you are going to speak to:

1. Introduction
    Your first name, last initial
    Identification as relative or friend of an alcoholic
    Request for respect of anonymity (reasons in relation to yourself and the alcoholic, particularly if in AA)
2. Al-Anon
    What it is
    How it Works: Knowledge of alcoholism results in more objective attitude toward the alcoholic
       Fellowship with others sharing the same problem
       Spiritual and emotional growth
3. Personal Recovery Stories from your own or others' experience
    How you found Al-Anon
    Personal serenity
    Getting back to mainstream of life
    Improvement of family morale, including children
    Impact, if any on the alcoholic

4. Future Cooperation: How to get in touch with Al-Anon or Alateen

Why referrals can be helpful to the family of the alcoholic, to the alcoholic and the group being addressed

Point 3—*how to say it.*

If you have memorized (or written down) only the high spots of your talk in brief notes, you will find you speak with much more ease than if you tried to follow a prepared script.

Speak slowly. If you habitually talk fast, deliberately slow yourself down; it will make you easier to understand, because it takes your hearers time to absorb ideas that are unfamiliar to them.

If possible, begin and end on a story, or a phrase that will stick in your hearer's minds.

These few rules will help you overcome the nervousness that besets even the most experienced speakers. As a great President of the U.S. once said about a talk he was about to give at his graduation: "I know more about what I'm going to talk about than any of *them* do, so they have more reason to be nervous than I have. So I just won't be!" This worked for F.D.R., a great orator. Try it; it will work for you, too.